New Minorities,
Old Conflicts

Asian and West Indian
Migrants in Britain

ETHNIC GROUPS IN COMPARATIVE
PERSPECTIVE • General Editor
PETER I. ROSE *Smith College*

Random House New York

New Minorities, Old Conflicts

Asian and West Indian Migrants in Britain

Sheila Allen
University of Bradford
Yorkshire, England

ISBN: 0-394-31477-8

Library of Congress Catalog Card Number: 78-132471

Manufactured in the United States of America. Composed by The Book Press, Inc., Brattleboro, Vt. Printed and bound by Halliday Lithograph, Inc. West Hanover, Mass.

Designed by Karin Batten

First Edition

987654321

For my parents, John and Marjorie McKenny

◉ Foreword

Not long ago I had occasion to spend a month in Kyoto, Japan, teaching about the ethnic characteristics of, and problems in, the United States and learning something of Japan's. The members of the "invisible race," known to westerners by the outmoded word Eta, were becoming visible and, to some, quite troublesome.

I told my students, mostly fellow professors, that I wanted to learn more about the situation and, after some negotiating, was able to make contact with the local leaders of the Buraku Emancipation movement. We spent hours together as I sought to get some sense of their status and their plight. While sitting there talking, drinking beer, and comparing impressions of my country and theirs, I had a strange sense of déjà vu.

My mind kept wandering back to October 1964, to a pub in the midlands of England where, in a not too dissimilar setting, Sheila Allen and several West Indian friends, all members of the newly formed Leicester Campaign for Racial Equality, were filling me in on the British racial scene. That earlier meeting, in a very real sense, was where this book began. (Perhaps, in the near future, my Japanese colleagues will have a similar volume on the Buraku ready for publication in this series.)

Sheila Allen's book is the second in this series to take readers beyond the borders of America. The first was Professor R. A. Schermerhorn's *Comparative Ethnic Relations*, a monumental work in which a number of theoretical problems were discussed and analyzed and suggestions for comparative study were offered. Because the author's manuscript was being prepared almost simultaneously, she did not have access to Schermerhorn's work. Yet, it should soon be apparent to readers of both volumes that she shares Schermerhorn's concern over the dearth of good comparative analysis in the field of racial and ethnic relations and shares his desire to rectify this through a far more dialectical approach.

In five detailed chapters Mrs. Allen sets her problem in its broader milieu. She recounts the history of "colored immigration" to Great Britain, paying special attention to both the centrifugal and centripetal forces prompting the movement, and she discusses the means set up to regulate the flow of immigration. The social organization of the principal new minorities in the country, the Asians from India and Pakistan and the West Indians, are examined. The author discusses intergroup relations with special reference to education and employment, and, finally, offers a comprehensive portrait of "a society in transition."

For British readers, she has placed page one problems into a meaningful context, and for Americans, she has drawn attention to the fact that what we are experiencing at home has many parallels elsewhere. For others, such as the Australians with whom I am currently working, Sheila Allen offers a sober assessment of deep-rooted prejudices and widespread patterns of resistance and reaction that have implications far beyond Westminster.

All told, this book is a welcome addition to this series and to the growing literature on ethnic relations in comparative perspective.

PETER I. ROSE
General Editor

The Flinders University of South Australia
September, 1970.

◉ Preface

This book attempts to explain some of the main aspects of the impact of colored immigration to Britain from parts of the Commonwealth, particularly during the past decade. It examines some of the principal approaches to immigration and race relations and endeavors to evaluate these in terms of the British situation. Explanations in which either the immigrant-host or colored-white aspects are emphasized do not lead to a useful understanding of the situation. Such an understanding, as I attempt to show, must be based on a structural analysis of British society. It is from within this society, seen in a historical and comparative perspective, that such terms as immigrant and color derive their meaning and relevance for social action. I am indebted to Peter I. Rose for his encouragement and interest. I discussed with him many of the aspects of the British situation when he was Visiting Professor of Sociology at the University of Leicester. My thanks are also due to Harold Wolpe, who read and criticized this study in its early stages, and with whom I have had many discussions about methodological questions.

Many others have contributed to this study in a variety of ways and I am grateful to them. Two, in particular, Stuart Bentley and Gurnam Sanghera, have given invaluable help.

I should also like to thank Joanna Bornat for her assistance in checking references and quotations, and I owe a special thanks to Gloria Bayley, Janet Wright, and Ann Lane, who, with patient good humor, undertook the typing of the manuscript.

The completion of the book was due to the constant support and encouragement of my husband, Vic.

SHEILA ALLEN

Bradford, Yorkshire, England

ix

◉ Contents

New Minorities, Old Conflicts

Asian and West Indian Migrants in Britain

Chapter 1 ◉ Sociological Approaches to Race Relations

The arrival in Britain of several hundred thousand people from India, Pakistan, and the West Indies over a comparatively short time evoked a variety of responses, which may be described as an emergent race-relations situation. Conditions in Britain do not as yet present the intractable difficulties which arise out of longstanding, inflexible and prejudiced attitudes, designed segregation, or consciously sought discrimination that do characterize racial situations in many parts of the world, notably South Africa, Rhodesia, and the United States.[1] However, Britain does not present the tolerant good will and understanding, regardless of color, race, or creed, expressed so frequently when prefacing statements on "immigrant problems." Often this myth of English tolerance is used to cover uncertainty, confusion, or discriminatory behavior. Race and race consciousness have emerged as factors to be reckoned with in countless situations in Britain. Politicians, administrators, employers, trade unionists, social workers, teachers, and many others express views, define problems, and take action with regard to "race" in the course of everyday situations. Whether race will become a dominant structural feature of British society is uncertain. In any event, the question cannot be answered without investigating the causes and consequences of social relationships involving people from the West Indies, India, Pakistan, and Great Britain within the British structural context.*

---

* The word "colored," as used in Britain, includes migrants from Africa, Asia, the Caribbean, and some from the Middle East, as well as the native British born of nonwhite or mixed parentage. The word, therefore, applies to people of many differing ethnic origins and backgrounds.

RACE AND RACE DIFFERENCES

Race is a term often misused, and misunderstanding of racial differences is common. Most people assume that differences of a racial character are fairly simple and obvious. The general observation that the world's population is divided into large groups, sharing similar physical characteristics, has led to many attempts at classifying these groups more rigorously as well as distinguishing subcategories within them. Although skin color or hair form differentiates between large groups, in general the gradations within the groups and the overlapping between them necessitate the use of additional criteria in order to produce a scientifically useful categorization. Subclassification of the species *Homo sapiens*, to which all human beings belong, using data on extinct as well as existent populations in different parts of the world, has proved difficult and exhibits a complexity ignored in the everyday usage of the term "race." A race, in the scientific use of the term, is distinguished from another race in terms of a complex of physical features that are transmitted genetically from one generation to the next. However, understanding of the processes of genetic transmission is neither exact nor complete. Any single characteristic, taken as an index of race, is not necessarily transmitted by a single gene but by combinations of genes, thus increasing the complexity of the problem. When we are dealing with more than one characteristic, the possibility of inheriting one but not the other is a further complication. The valuable work of biologists and physical anthropologists has shown the possibilities and the present limitations of a scientific classification of races.[2]

When such classifications are applied to actual living human beings further problems arise due, among other things, to the movements and interbreeding of populations for many thousands of years. The racial, physical characteristics attributed to any one group are averages or norms. For instance, one classification divides the world's population into Caucasian, Mongoloid, and Negroid races: the Caucasian, more commonly thought of as European, generally speaking has light skin, but some do have darker skins than those in the other groups. In addition to the overlapping between these groups, the variety within any one group is considerable. In Europe, for example, three subtypes have been identified: Nordic, Alpine, and Mediterranean. Attempts have been made to classify actual populations in accordance with these subtypes. However, populations in Europe exhibit such a mixture that classification into the three types cannot be made to correlate accurately with any national group and much less with any particular individual European, who may, indeed, possess characteristics from any of the three types. For instance, investigations of the physical characteristics of the population of Sweden showed that only a minority could be described as "Nordic," that is, having fair hair, light eyes, long skulls, and tall stature.[3] Pure types, then, remain tentative classifications which will function only as a convenient aid in exploring the historical origins of populations. They, therefore, are not descriptions of existing populations where a heterogeneity of physical characteristics is commonly found.

The gap between scientific attempts at precise classifications and everyday usage is wide when race is used in reference not only to biologically transmissible qualities but also to differences that are social in character. The confusion of religious, national, or linguistic groups with racial groups is scientifically incorrect. In terms of intergroup relations, members of such religious or national groups may describe themselves and be judged by others as belonging to separate races. The distinction between Aryans and non-Aryans in Nazi Germany was not a scientific exercise concerned with different linguistic groupings, to which Aryan strictly refers, but a division on a supposed racial basis. In many situations, this idea of race has been a powerful differentiating mechanism and, as such, is the concern of the social scientist.

Furthermore, it is common to attribute different ways of life and thought to racial differences and to assume that differences in mental abilities and aptitudes are explained by race. The assertion that some races have lower intelligence than others, accepted as self-evident by many, has been subjected to considerable attention by social investigators. The question of comparative intelligence is not a simple one to answer. Psychologists using verbal and nonverbal tests on different groups produce results relating to the groups tested. These results are open to both misinterpretation and misunderstanding. The misinterpretation centers around popular notions that group scores can be applied to individuals. So if in a particular investigation white Americans score higher than black Americans, this then tells us about average scores for groups but does not mean a white American will score higher than a black American. The reverse can be, and often is, the case. Group scores are not directly correlative with individual performance or potential.

The misunderstanding of investigations of comparative testing arises from assumptions about intelligence and intelligence-testing techniques. Psychologists have developed tests that can be considered valid within known limits, when used under specified conditions. When they are used under other conditions, the validity of the results is not known. One of the most difficult tasks in comparative work has been the development of tests that are valid cross-culturally.[4]

In verbal tests the problems of language are obvious. Nonverbal tests, in which problem solving is required through handling of wood blocks and jigsaws, manipulating simple pictures, and the like have been designed to overcome some of the disadvantages of verbal testing. It has not yet been possible to develop tests that isolate intelligence from the effects of educational environment, socioeconomic influences, and cultural experience. Therefore, the results of cross-cultural testing relate not only to intelligence but also, to an unknown extent, to the other factors involved. Performance differences among races in intelligence-test scores can be due to any of these other factors. If greater refinements in techniques are devised, it may be possible to construct ways of isolating intelligence differences in terms of the social or biological correlates.[5] The kind of society in which an individual grows up affects his behavior. Thinking, planning, recognizing, and remembering are intricately interrelated with the totality of the individual's experience. Mental differences, both qualitatively and quantitatively, have not yet been investigated in such a way as to show clearly how potentialities and abilities are molded and developed by social influences. Consequently, to attribute differential performance to genetic differences is to fail to confront the problem of comparative mental development in its social context. The assertion that differential performance is attributable to skin color, shape of head, or stature, and the like neglects existing evidence to the contrary. In assessing the relations between races, however, what is important is not simply the state of our knowledge, as determined by the cautious investigations and tentative discussions of biologists, physical anthropologists, and psychologists but the ways in which those relations are defined in everyday life. As W. I. Thomas has written, "If men define situations as real, they are real in their consequences."[6] When white men define black men as inferior this will affect the way the white men treat them, which in turn influences the development and responses of the black men.[7]

Other characteristics are frequently described as due to racial differences. Poverty, overcrowding, low levels of educational aspiration, and work habits are a few factors believed by many to be racial in origin. Correlations may often exist between one or more of these factors and some groups with similar, visible physical characteristics. It is, however, erroneous to relate causally skin color or head form with overcrowding or lack of success.[8] The sociological significance of such correlations rests on sociocultural conditions and not on biological determinants. John Stuart Mill once wrote: "Of all the vulgar modes of escaping from the consideration of the effect of social and moral influences on the human mind, the most vulgar is that of attributing diversities of conduct and character to inherent natural differences."[9]

RACE AS A SOCIAL PROBLEM

Much of the work that deals with ethnic and racial groups has, perhaps inevitably, concentrated on social problems. This has had an important influence not only on particular investigations, but more significantly, from our point of view, on the general framework within which race relations are examined. Where practical matters have predominated, race relations have been defined as problem relations, and solutions have been sought. This manner of viewing race relations has consequences for investigations and policy recommendations. The focus has been situationally specific and the more general questions of race relations, in their structural and comparative aspects, neglected. The necessity of offering solutions has meant the incorporation of value assumptions about ideal social relations and the means of achieving these. Furthermore, because of the dominance of social-work "case method theories" within the field of social problems, the emphasis has been largely on individual solutions to individual problems. Where social conflict and social disorganization are recognized, the problem center has become the minority or immigrant group, and solutions have been seen in terms of adaptation by such groups to the dominant culture; failure of the immigrant or minority group to adapt or adjust is then explained in terms of the group's characteristics. Currently this focus is widely held in Britain by social workers, educationalists, politicians, and many professionally concerned with immigrant groups. In analyzing the causes and consequences of intergroup relations and in examining the developmental aspects of these relations, a problem-solving perspective obscures many of the substantive questions that need investigation. Race relations is not an individual problem, resolvable by individual action, nor is it a problem to be understood by reference to the characteristics of simply one racial group. Although we may or may not approve of action to solve some race problem, we must recognize that, unless action is based on knowledge of the structure and processes of intergroup relations, it is likely to be self-deating. Further complications arise from the moral approval or disapproval associated with inter-ethnic relations. The failure to distinguish between the dynamics of prejudice and the mechanisms of conformity leads to endless confusion, not only in discourse but also in much research and practical work.[10] There are dangers in drawing conclusions about prejudice from data that may indicate nothing more than conformity to what are believed to be widely held, and thus acceptable, views. For the social scientist the question is: Under what conditions and by what means do prejudicial statements about minority groups become the norm to which members of the majority group conform? In addition, the extent to which the majority group internalizes prejudice warrants careful investigation.

RACE AND SOCIAL STRUCTURE

In many situations differences of religion, nationality, culture, and color have been viewed as indications of racial differences and have been used to accord differential treatment to the individuals and groups so labeled. For the sociologist, the general question to be raised and examined is: Under what conditions are differences perceived as relevant and how do processes of inclusion and exclusion emerge and operate? Many concepts and hypotheses, centered on specific situations or, more usually, specific characteristics of particular groups, have been developed in attempts to clarify the causes and consequences of race relations. In recent years, attention has been directed toward examining race relations as one element within a total system of social relations. This approach is more fruitful in sociological explanation than considering race and racial differences as entities separate from the structures within which race relations develop and from which they take their form and content. In brief, the structural context of economic, political, and social institutions is the key to the social definition of racial distinctions or racial identity. This and the following chapters will show that it is within these contexts that the sociological significance of race is to be found.

Milton M. Gordon, who writes about race relations in the United States, outlines a similar approach. He says, "We shall concern ourselves with what, to my mind, is the equally important [to racial discrimination and hostility], logically prior, and substantially neglected problem of *the nature of group life itself* within a large, industrialised, urban nation."[11] He explains the general neglect of this approach in terms of the concern with immediate practical problems, the traditional emphasis on personality and attitude dynamics in studies of prejudice, and the stress on cultural behavior in relation to the dominant American value system. This has led to minimal attention being given to ". . . the social structure of our racial, religious, and national groups and their various interrelationships."[12] He considers that without analyses ". . . *in terms of the crucial considerations of social structure* . . ." a worker investigating intergroup relations is like a horse without blinkers. "He doesn't know where he's been, he doesn't know where he is and he doesn't know where he's going."[13]

The term "minority group" is rarely used in Britain, although it is more useful than many other concepts when describing the position of colored immigrants in British social structure. The term has been used by sociologists to refer to groups whose members share racial or ethnic similarities that are thought to be different from or inferior to the characteristics of the dominant group and, as a result, are treated differently and unequally.[14] It does not refer to a statistical minority. The groups so described may form a majority of the population within a given society or region. This is the case in South Africa or Rhodesia, for instance, where the people of European stock form the dominant structural group; whereas those of African descent, though much more numerous, form a sociological minority.

The dominant group in Britain consists of white-skinned people who, at least nominally, are Christians. The patterns of behavior, language, moral standards, and customs that are thought to make up the "British way of life" derive from within it. It is this group who generally determine who shall be minorities and so create and perpetuate minority status. The dominant group is, however, highly differentiated internally. Those in positions of economic and political power are drawn from this group, but, of course, not all members occupy such positions. In a very important sense, however, they are members of the dominant group, vis-à-vis the colored population.

When race relations in Britain are under consideration, two aspects of the dominant structure must be kept in mind: the high degree of internal differentiation and the process of rapid transition that the society has undergone and is still experiencing. Members of the dominant structure are marked by certain shared characteristics, that is, they are white, nominally Protestant Christians, literate, urbanized, and involved in industrial occupations. However, these do not provide the basis of a simple cohesion maintained by a set of common values. The structure is permeated with different customs and styles of life, and different beliefs and ways of behaving derived from generational and class experience. A host of subgroups marked by the influence of region, educational opportunity, political affiliation, and occupational position characterize British society. On close examination there are many "British ways of life," not just one. The notion that there is only one is an ideological, rather than a structural, reality. The influence of this ideology is relevant to the analysis of race relations, but it should not be mistaken for a description of how the British live.

The urban and rural differences, so important in many societies, are of little significance in Britain. Almost 60 percent of the population live in towns of more than 50,000.[15] The rural population, because of the ease and speed of communication, is influenced by urban ways of living and thought. Despite a nostalgia for, and an idealization of, rural life, few experience this life and fewer have their lives shaped by it.

Regional ties are of greater significance. Many regional differences involve traditional enmities and loyalties, evoking feelings of identity and exclusion. Stereotyped images of Yorkshiremen and Cornish men, East Anglians, Mancunians (from Manchester), and Cockneys (from London) are held not only by others but also by the natives of these regions. The geographical and social mobility, which has been such an important feature of British life for the past two centuries, has removed most of the actual differences. Of those remaining, dialect and accent are perhaps the most marked. Geographical mobility does less to remove these than social mobility. Standardized or "Oxford" English is valued more highly than regional accents and so the educational system places stress on the acquisition of this accent or a near imitation. Although differences in speech are noticeable from region to region, within any one region there will be further differences according to social class.

Divisions within the white population along national and religious lines have been extremely important historically, and some of these persist. The Scots, Welsh, and, more especially, the Irish have retained indigenous customs and, in some cases, language differences. They possess different educational systems and have inherited and perpetuate a different intellectual culture. The Irish were long thought by the English to be incapable of self-government because of their "Celtic blood." Recent developments in national consciousness have been expressed in Scotland and Wales in demands for self-government. The extent to which these groups continue a separate way of life tends to be overlooked by those who claim that there was an integrated British society until the arrival of colored immigrants.[16] Jews, despite their long settlement in Britain and the "Anglicizing" of much of their behavior, are regarded not only as a separate religious group but also as racially different.[17] Cypriots, Greeks, Italians, and Poles are among recent examples of people who, at least in the first generation, occupy minority status.* There is some evident degree of cultural diversity in Britain, but this does not produce a plural society of equal and competing groups.† Cultural diversity is related to a dominant and minority structure within which the dominant structure controls the legal, economic, political, and educational systems, each of which can encroach on areas of cultural diversity and limit them directly or indirectly. As a result of religious or national differences, some groups occupy minority status and, at the same time, are in a dominant structural position vis-à-vis the colored population.

Stratification, a further differentiation, marks social relation-

---

* Attacks on the property of residents, some of them longstanding British citizens bearing Italian names, took place on the outbreak of the war with Italy in 1940. Although an extreme situation, this behavior demonstrates the latent divisions on ethnic grounds.

† The term "plural" society was first used to characterize those societies, in a colonial situation, composed of different ethnic groups in which intergroup relations were entered into in the market but separate ways of life were maintained outside this limited contact.[18] When the term is applied to other societies, where groups are differentiated by conflicting interests, different values, and a relative absence of crosscutting ties between groups, the term then becomes too broad, virtually useless. Unless the degree of differentiation necessary to constitute the society as "plural" is specified and the institutional bases of pluralism distinguished, it becomes possible to call all complex societies "plural," when what is really meant is internal structural differentiation. Cultural pluralism, though not used consistently or unambiguously, indicates diversity in language, marriage and family customs, religious affiliation, dress, and eating habits.

ships in Britain to a greater degree than any of the differentiations thus far discussed. The complexity and subtlety of this stratification indicates the need for a separation of the component parts of the system. In this way, the degrees of autonomy of the parts and the manner of their interrelations can be understood. The term "class" is frequently used to indicate not only economic position but also status level, relative power and prestige, and subjective evaluations of individuals and groups. When the term is used in this manner, it has little or no explanatory value in discussions of social relationships; it includes everything and explains nothing.[19] Conversely, the tendency to equate stratification solely with economic divisions neglects the importance of accepted social distinctions, including race, which may, in some circumstances, override economic differences. The British class structure, viewed in terms of the material position of groups differentiated by their access to goods and services, is primarily defined by the distribution of property. Within this definition, however, important structural distinctions must be made in terms of the type and amount of income.[20] Such differences are directly related to the chances of acquiring skills that command differential rewards.

Nonetheless, the acquisition and evaluation of skills are not only dependent on the demands of the economic order but also are related to the evaluations and processes of the social order. One of the most important aspects of the stratification system is the links existing between distribution of income, occupation, and education. Occupations carrying differential rewards, both economic and social, mark different styles of life. It is within these that Britons live their lives. One of the main determinants of social mobility is education, and the chances of acquiring a particular kind of education are largely the result of social origin. Class and status are not identical but are functionally interrelated: class position is legitimated by status exclusion, and status restrictions provide a means of monopolizing economic skills. This reciprocity and interpenetration is not static, nor is it symmetrical. In some situations the economic order predominates, in others, the social order. As Max Weber observed, "class distinctions are linked in the most varied ways with status distinctions."[21] When a status group acquires legal recognition of its position, it may use this in economic and political spheres to exclude other groups from legal access to positions within these spheres. It was supposed by Weber that in industrial societies such use of legal exclusion was not only uncommon but also contrary to the rationality involved in industrialism. Where, however, status distinctions based on racial or ethnic origins are involved, the legal order may be used to support and perpetuate distinctions by endowing some groups with rights and excluding others.

Class and status groups, differing in the amounts of power, skill, and prestige they command and in the values they accept, enter every aspect of British life. The structure of minority groups may be viewed from the perspective of Weber's status hierarchy. The characteristics of religion, national or ethnic origin, and race and color become part of the definition of social interaction, producing, under some circumstances, relatively exclusive groupings that are differentially evaluated. Furthermore, the internal differentiation of a status group must be considered in terms of general class and status hierarchies and not in isolation from them.

The complexities of British social structure are overlaid by her long history as the center of an overseas empire. Natives of Britain, from every social strata, have been involved in this Empire as capitalists, traders, missionaries, administrators, military and police personnel, and the like. These experiences have given rise to attitudes of paternalism and superiority toward colored people. White men from the most humble origins in Britain have found themselves in positions of power and prestige in relation to colored populations. Many schoolchildren still learn their history and geography from books that characterize the inhabitants of Commonwealth countries by derogatory stereotypes. With the struggle for national independence, open conflict has marked relations between the British and their colonial subjects in many areas and frequently military suppression has preceded political independence.

Moreover, the colonies, with their exploitable resources, both natural and human, played a significant part in the increasing prosperity in which the majority of Great Britain's inhabitants shared. As a result, there was a real conflict of interest between the standard of life in Britain and the growing demand for independence in the colonies. Long ago Joseph Chamberlain indicated this:

> Believe me, if . . . any change took place which deprived us of [that] control and influence . . . , the first to suffer would be the working men of the country . . . . If the working men of this country understood . . . their interests, they will not lend any countenance to the doctrines of those politicians who never lose an opportunity of pouring contempt and abuse upon the brave Englishmen, who . . . , in all parts of the world are carving out new dominions for Britain, and are opening up fresh markets for British commerce, and laying out fresh fields for British labour.[22]

This interrelation has become more obvious with the granting of independence and the change from Empire to Commonwealth.

In the British Labour movement, for instance, the traditional ideology of brotherhood crumbles before pressures on their own standard of living and the arrival of some of these "brothers" to the British labor market. The immigration policy becomes one of restriction rather than the open-door policy that marked Britain's relations with her overseas territories for so long. In 1951 a nationwide survey showed that half of the British people interviewed had never seen a colored person. However, the presence of about a million colored people in Britain in mid-1966 has demonstrated the legacy of a long history between Britain and the countries from which the colored immigrants come.[23] Now this interrelationship between Britain and her former Empire is being worked out, formally and informally, in the relations of colored and white at all levels of British society. It influences the attitudes and behavior of teachers and children, employers and employees, politicians and their constituents.

Structurally, the white population is highly differentiated in terms of class and status and social groups based on cultural, religious, and national differences that cut across economic divisions. The impact of colored immigration must be seen in light of this existing structure. Color is one important status dimension, but its significance varies with the situational aspects of intergroup relations. A West Indian doctor may be treated as a doctor or a black man, that is, in occupational or color terms. Status ambiguities arise in some situations; in others, a clear definition exists. Within the space of a few hours, or even minutes, an individual, having changed neither his occupation nor his color, only his situation, may be accorded prestige and respect and then refused food or drink or be unable to hire a taxi.

RACE AND SOCIAL PROCESS

Sociologists who concentrate on structural aspects are frequently criticized for reifying the structure of a society or group. This criticism is not without some foundation. Social reality involves both the external, objective, constraining structure and the subjective meanings of the individual actors. Activity is a product of both of these in dialectical interaction.[24] The previously mentioned illustration of the West Indian doctor demonstrates the need to examine the processes or mechanisms by which definitions and redefinitions of individuals, groups, and situations are intricately interwoven.

Many of the assumptions and conceptual tools used to analyze the processes of intergroup relations of an ethnic or racial character derive from the transatlantic migrations of the nineteenth and twentieth centuries and the Continental and Irish immigrations to Britain during the same period. Few sociologists would now go as far as Robert E. Park did when he asserted that "in the relations of races there is a cycle of events which tends everywhere to repeat itself."[25] His cycle of events involved the initial contact of differing groups, a period of competition followed by a process of accommodation, then assimilation or amalgamation. This obviously does not cover cases like that of Black Americans, who were inhabitants of the United States long before the majority of European immigrants, but are still in a structurally inferior position. Nor does it account for those members of the colored population who have been in Britain for several generations and now find themselves and their children classed as immigrants. However, many of the concepts derived from "cycles" of race relations are still accepted and used in Britain.

The vocabulary of concepts has been clearly influenced by proposed solutions of racial problems. For instance, the term "assimilation," as developed by H. P. Fairchild and Robert E. Park, carried physiological connotations and was an inevitable one-way process leading to total identity with the host group. Park regarded the term as:

> . . . merely the more generic and abstract concept for which Americanization and the verbs Americanize, Anglicize and Germanize are more specific terms. All these words are intended to describe the process by which the generally accepted social customs and political ideas and loyalties of a community or country are transmitted to an adopted citizen.[26]

This concept can be directly traced to the "Americanization" policy during and after World War I when conformity was identified with the national interest and patriotism; in fact, the idea is much older. Milton M. Gordon comments that "it is quite likely that 'Anglo-conformity' in its more moderate forms has been, . . . the most prevalent ideology of assimilation in America throughout the nation's history."[27] Assimilation remained as a central concept long after the policy of forced cultural conformity had fallen into disrepute and numerous studies had shown that ethnic groups within the United States persisted for generations without assimilating. Modifications were made to allow assimilation to mean a two-way process of adaptation. The time span was altered from years to generations and the notion of accommodation introduced. In addition, variations in the processes were allowed for, so that, for example, the notion of overall uniformity was replaced by ". . . economic absorption but cultural pluralism; cultural absorption at some levels . . . yet cultural differentiation and isolation at others."[28]

Implicit in assimilation was the assumption that the structure and habits of migrant groups change sufficiently for them to become part of the structure of the society into which they have moved. Short of total conformity, it was never possible to determine how much change was sufficient. In cases where external visibility was a factor, complete conformity was hardly a viable aim; if it was to retain any meaning, the term "assimilation" could not be used in such situations. Black Americans could not be said to have assimilated after 300 years, however American they might be, whereas second generation Italians, Poles, Lithuanians, and Irish could be said to have assimilated on a behavioral level, since they were not externally distinguishable and retained few of the distinctive cultural traits of their immigrant forebears. Nonetheless, it is a very different matter when the in-group solidarity of such groups is analyzed. Studies of second and subsequent generations of externally assimilated ethnic groups show wide variations in their degree of conformity. The work of William Foot Whyte in the 1930s and Herbert J. Gans in the late 1950s demonstrates the ethnic inclusiveness of social contact and institutional participation of second generation Italian-Americans.[29] A study of intermarriage of groups of various national origins and religious affiliations, over a period of eighty years, 1870–1950, illustrates that the rates of intermarriage, though declining, were still high at the end of the period. In the study half of those of Irish descent married others of their own national origin, and three-quarters of Italian descent married Italian-Americans.[30] Information on two generations of Norwegians in a prairie town and a prairie farming community shows how assimilation may proceed at different rates in different spheres and the extent to which the original cultural background may be retained. In religion, choice of marriage partners, and economic relations being of Norwegian stock was extremely important, but less so in the economic sphere than in marriage. Moreover, the study showed that in face-to-face contact with non-Norwegians little understanding was displayed of the norms and motives of the outgroup.[31] The maintenance of an in-group identity, in this case, where the group is neither physically distinguishable nor relegated to an inferior structural position, calls into question the usefulness of the assimilation concept.

Assimilation may be applied to individuals of diverse ethnic origins who become, for all intents and purposes, members of the dominant social and cultural groups. This is not merely a matter of choice, of willingness to change on the part of the individual, but it is highly dependent on the attitudes of the host society. Skin color or alien religious allegiance, for instance, may prevent such a transition. Even the assimilation of individuals is not an irreversible process. This was demonstrated in a most extreme form in Germany and occupied Europe during the Nazi era, when those with even remote Jewish origins were actively sought out for persecution.

In recent years, the term "assimilation," though still used by some, has been increasingly replaced, both in public discourse and academic work, by the term "integration."* This change is due partly to the recognition that total conformity is the exception rather than the normal process and also to the undesirability or inadvisability of demanding such conformity. In short, assimilation carries value connotations that it is now felt are best discarded.

Integration does not imply a laissez-faire approach, and voluntary segregation is not encouraged. Integration aims at achieving ". . . uniformity where this is felt to be necessary in the interests of the receiving society and cultural pluralism where this is essential to the welfare of the immigrant."[33] Such a definition neither specifies who decides the limits of uniformity, how these are to be imposed, nor the range of cultural diversity that is regarded as acceptable. One of the crucial questions in intergroup relations concerns the power to demand conformity: By whom and for whom is it felt to be essential? The older concept of assimilation clearly demands change from the immigrant, so that he and his group can be incorporated wholly into the dominant way of life. Assimilation also specifies limits as to those who can be considered assimilable. Integration, on the other hand, demands some unspecified degree of change, the limits of which are made explicit in an ad hoc manner only. Because the bulk of legal, economic, political, and customary sanctions lies in the hands of dominant groups, these decisions are not made between equally contending parties. If

---

* "Absorption" is also used, though more rarely. S. N. Eisenstadt uses the term very much the same way others use integration. His major concepts of adaptation or absorption and role aspirations of immigrants clearly focus on the individual. The central concern is the personality equilibrium of the individual.[32]

integration is seen as a balance of interests of the host society and the welfare of the immigrants, this would then assume that common interests exist between host society and a homogeneous immigrant group sharing welfare needs. In the context of a complex industrial society with diverse migrant groups, these are problematic assumptions and further assumptions are frequently incorporated. "This concept of integration rests upon a belief in the importance of cultural differentiation within a framework of social unity. It recognizes the rights of groups and individuals to be different so long as the differences do not lead to domination or disunity."[34] If allowable differences are not meant to lead to domination, then it must be assumed that domination does not exist. However, this is not congruent with the accumulated evidence of migrations.[35] Race-relations situations are not merely circumstances in which all start equal, though different. Social disunity can be produced either by immigrants who go beyond the "limits of diversity" or by host groups who attempt to maintain their dominant position by defining and excluding immigrants. Until the term "integration" is more carefully specified, many might agree with the sentiments of the British Home Secretary, who in 1967 defined it ". . . not as a flattening process of assimilation, but as equal opportunity accompanied by cultural diversity in an atmosphere of mutual tolerance."[36] Nonetheless, this definition is not useful for understanding the social processes involved in intergroup relations.

For analytical purposes the limits of autonomy or separateness and the degrees of interdependence or integration considered necessary for the maintenance of an ongoing social system must be outlined. This question of autonomy and interdependence of parts of a system remains one of the most difficult and crucial problems in sociology. It is resolved neither by assuming away the difficulties nor by pretending that in relations between ethnic or racial groups integration takes on a special, known and accepted meaning that it does not have for other intergroup relations. For example, one of the difficulties in understanding the term, using it as an analytical tool, or translating it into practical action is the confusion between the different levels to which it is applied. It is used when referring to individual interaction, relationships, and societal or system processes. Individual examples of "integration" are put forward to disprove discrimination against the racial group, so that the existence of one black teacher in a school or one black policeman in a city is frequently cited in opposition to claims that institutional discrimination is practiced. Nonetheless, institutional and individual integration are not the same thing. If, in order to get certain positions, applicants with black skins have to be better qualified than white applicants, or if most black people cannot gain the necessary qualifications to compete in the first place, then the basis of institutional integration is lacking. A high degree of integration at one level does not preclude absence of integrative processes at other levels. Moreover, integration is not without its cost. The Indians living in Britain, "who keep open house and share food, money and accommodation, who rally to each other's aid in times of sickness, death or trouble," comment, "You keep talking about integrating us . . . . Why don't you integrate yourselves?"[37] A high level of village-kin integration, lacking among urban white groups, is, however, not what is meant when integration of immigrants is discussed. This kind of integration within one group may well prove incompatible with integration into the dominant economic, political, and social structure of Britain. To include in the term "integration" the complex and variable processes involved in intergroup relations obscures understanding of these relationships and creates an inability to deal with the consequences.

Much of the basic information regarded by social scientists as crucial for delineating and investigating relationships between colored and white groups does not exist in Britain. The overall size of the colored population, its sex, age, and social composition are known in the broadest outline only. These factors are considered in greater detail in later chapters. However, one further aspect of the present situation will be discussed.

IMMIGRATION AND RACE RELATIONS

The immigrant status of the majority of Britain's colored population complicates the situation. The problems have been identified largely in terms of immigrant-host relationships rather than colored-white relationships.[38] This has been referred to as "the hallowed view that our race relations problems are at bottom immigrant problems."[39] In an investigation of West Indians in Britain, Mrs. Patterson represents the situation in these terms: ". . . what we have in Britain at the present stage is not, or not yet, basically a colour or a race situation, however much it may appear so to many colour-conscious migrants—it is an immigrant situation."[40] She goes on to specify that the situation is complicated by the color factor and that West Indians, West Africans, and Asians are viewed more immediately in the following way:

> . . . visible and more strange . . . than the thousands of other immigrants who have entered the country since the Second World War. But the difference is at present one of degree rather than of kind. In Britain—that insular, conservative, homogeneous society—mild xenophobia or antipathy to outsiders would appear a cultural norm. It is extended in varying degrees to all outsiders, to Poles and to coloured people, and to people from the next village or street.[41]

The immigrant status of many of the colored population can be compared, in many respects, to that of other immigrants, such as the Irish, Poles, and Italians. As immigrants they share the designation of outsiders, their relationships to the host society tend to be marginal, and they face common problems of adjustment to a new way of life. Often they come from rural agricultural areas to live and work in urban industrial situations; moreover, they bring with them religious and cultural beliefs and behavior patterns alien to those of the host society. In spite of this, it is not only in terms of their immigrant characteristics that the response of the white host society is structured. It is not the "color-conscious migrant" alone who defines the situation; the color-conscious host also plays a part. Structurally, the whites are dominant in cultural, political, and economic terms; therefore, their definition of the situation is likely to be a major determinant in the development of white-black relations.

At the present time it is not possible to say that color is *the* dominant factor structuring social relations, nor would such an assumption prove very useful. Theories of race relations that assume color to be the explanatory variable ignore other differentiating elements present in the situation that may be of equal or greater significance. Indeed, the question should be: How far is color seen as a relevant means of differentiating between groups within the society? If exclusion and suspicion of all outsiders is a general cultural characteristic of the English, then the question becomes: How do outsiders become ingroup members and under what conditions do they remain outsiders for long or relatively short periods? Lloyd Warner and Leo Srole, along with many sociologists concerned with ethnic and racial relations in America, believe that ". . . when the combined cultural and biological traits are highly divergent from those of the host society the subordination of the group will be very great, their subsystem strong, the period of assimilation long, and the processes slow and usually painful."[42] Findings of recent investigations in Britain suggest that although immigrant characteristics are frequently advanced as explanations of the differential treatment of colored groups, in the case of those members of colored groups with the *fewest* such characteristics, this treatment is still extended and its application increased.[43] A child born in Britain of West Indian-born, colored parents is regarded by many education authorities as an immigrant, whereas a bilingual child of Polish-born parents is not. Although some jobs, largely those connected with defense, are barred to children of foreign white immigrants, still they do not face the same problems of discrimination that the English-born, English-educated, colored children usually experience when they apply for employment. According to the valuations of the host society, the marginality of first-generation immigrants may be similar for all groups, differing only in degree. If, however, color is defined as a characteristic for differentiation, color then has the potential of permanency and so becomes a difference of kind. The situation in Britain must be assessed in the light of this possibility.

Comparative studies of the experiences of different immigrant groups in Britain is fruitful for assessing the significance of immigrant status relative to that of religious, ethnic, or color differences. Two aspects are especially relevant: the temporary or permanent character of these attributes and the processes by which each yields to redefinition within given frameworks of social relations. Patterns of immigrant-host relationships and inter-ethnic or color contacts are the product of a wide variety of influences. The development of any specific set must be viewed in several ways: the immediate elements (the characteristics of host and immigrant, for example), the wider context of structural changes in the receiving society, and the redefinitions of color or ethnicity in international relations. It cannot be assumed, for instance, that patterns of immigrant-host relationships inevitably repeat themselves.[44] This would ignore the relevance of changes, which may have taken place within the host society, and would neglect the developments in relations between societies. It has been suggested that possibly the "entire nature of race and ethnic relations has changed with the passing of colonialism and the rise of nationalism."[45] Some immigrants to Britain are never regarded as such; but others retain this status indefinitely, and some acquire immigrant status because of their color, though they are not, in fact, immigrants. In order to understand intergroup relations, comparisons of experience are useful, although these cannot be wholly confined to studies of other immigrant groups. The dynamic relation between social structure and racial attitudes and behavior involves an analysis of comparative and historical material that is necessary for any theory of intergroup relations.[46] The task is then to locate these relations within a structural context, taking into account the processes by which they emerge and are maintained.

Notes

[1] For a general though oversimplified view of world race relations, see Ronald Segal, *The Race War* (London: Jonathan Cape, 1966).

[2] For a longer discussion of this aspect, see Raymond Firth, *Human Types* (New York: Mentor Books, 1958), pp. 13–37.

[3] *Ibid.*, pp. 20–21.

[4] Gordon W. Allport, *The Nature of Prejudice* (New York: Anchor Books, 1958), pp. 89–90.

5 Researches relating to group differences will be found, among others, in the following: T. R. Garth, *Race Psychology* (New York: McGraw-Hill, 1931); O. Klineberg, *Race Differences* (New York: Harper & Row, 1935); Anne Anastasi and J. P. Foley, *Differential Psychology* (New York: Macmillan, 1949).

6 Morris Janowitz (ed.), *W. I. Thomas on Social Organization and Social Personality, Selected Papers* (Chicago: University of Chicago Press, 1966), p. 301.

7 For further discussion of responses to inferior status, see Brewton Berry, *Race and Ethnic Relations,* 3rd ed. (Boston: Houghton Mifflin, 1965) especially Chap. 16; George E. Simpson and J. Milton Yinger, *Racial and Cultural Minorities,* rev. ed. (New York: Harper & Row, 1958).

8 For a discussion of racial beliefs, see Simpson and Yinger, *op. cit.*, pp. 41–48.

9 Oliver C. Cox, *Caste, Class and Race* (New York: Doubleday, 1948), p. 537.

10 Percy Black and Ruth D. Atkins, "Conformity versus Prejudice Exemplified in White-Negro Relations in the South: Some Methodological Considerations," *Journal of Psychology,* 30 (July 1950), 109–121.

11 Milton M. Gordon, *Assimilation in American Life* (New York: Oxford University Press, 1964), p. 3. Italics in original.

12 *Ibid.*, p. 4.

13 *Ibid.*, p. 9.

14 Donald Young, *American Minority Peoples* (New York: Harper & Row, 1932); Louis Wirth, "The Problems of Minority Groups," in Ralph Linton (ed.), *The Science of Man in the World of Crisis* (New York: Columbia University Press, 1945).

15 General Register Office, *Census, 1961, England and Wales, Preliminary Report* (London: H.M.S.O. [Her Majesty's Stationery Office], 1961), p. 14.

16 See the arguments put forward in Normal Pannell and Fenner Brockway, *Immigration, What is the Answer?* (London: Routledge and Kegan Paul, 1965), pp. 36–42.

17 An interesting comment on the ethnic divisions in British life emerges in the following: ". . . the debate . . . over Rachman and 'rachmanism' at no time came to centre on his Jewish origins. Indeed, for some time, the Press referred to him not as a Jew but as a Pole. One can think of few other countries where, at a time of political trauma and noisy populism, such restraint would have

been shown." Poles living in Britain may not feel so sanguine about such treatment. The term "rachmanism" refers, among other things, to the exploitation and violent treatment of tenants by gangs employed by landlords and property owners in order to take over accommodation. Rachmanism is derived from the name Rachman, who was one such property owner. For a further discussion of the structure and social composition of the Jewish community, see Julius Gould and Shaul Esh (eds.), Jewish Life in Modern Britain (London: Routledge and Kegan Paul, 1964), p. 200.

[18] J. S. Furnivall, Colonial Policy and Practice, A Comparative Study of Burma and Netherlands India (New York: Cambridge University Press, 1948); B. Benedict, "Stratification in Plural Society," American Anthropologist, 64 (December 1962), 1235–1246; R. T. Smith, "Review of Social and Cultural Pluralism in the Caribbean," American Anthropologist, 63 (February 1961), 155–157; P. C. Van den Berghe, "Towards a Sociology of Africa," Social Forces, 43 (October 1964), 11–18; John Rex, "The Plural Society in Sociological Theory," British Journal of Sociology, 10 (June 1959), 114–124.

[19] For one of the most useful discussions of class and social stratification, see Stanislaw Ossowski, Class Structure in the Social Consciousness (London: Routledge and Kegan Paul, 1963).

[20] For the distribution of property and some of its social implications, see J. E. Meade, Efficiency, Equality and the Ownership of Property (London: G. Allen and Unwin, 1964), pp. 27–39. For income distribution, see Richard M. Titmuss, Income Distribution and Social Change (London: G. Allen and Unwin, 1962).

[21] H. H. Gerth and C. Wright Mills (eds.), From Max Weber: Essays in Sociology (London: Routledge and Kegan Paul, 1948), p. 187.

[22] "Want of Employment and the Development of Free Markets" (Birmingham: January 22, 1894), in Foreign and Colonial Speeches (London: J. Routledge & Sons, 1897), p. 133. Reproduced by permission.

[23] "Facts Paper, Colour and Immigration in the United Kingdom" (London: Institute of Race Relations, 1969), p. 2.

[24] The theoretical problems and research implications of this perspective are both complex and far-reaching, but they are not our immediate concern. For further discussion of this perspective, see Peter L. Berger and Thomas Luckmann, The Social Construction of Reality (London: Allen Lane, 1967). Also, see Alfred Schutz, Collected Papers, Vol. 1 (The Hague: Nijhoff, 1962). The analysis of race relations presented in this work owes much to this perspec-

tive but it can be regarded only as a preliminary treatment. The rigorous development of such a framework and its application to research remains an imperative task for students of race relations.

[25] Robert E. Park, *Race and Culture* (Glencoe, Illinois: Free Press, 1950), p. 150.

[26] H. P. Fairchild, Immigration, *A World Movement and Its American Significance*, rev. ed. (New York: Macmillan, 1925), p. 396 ff.; Park, *op. cit.*, pp. 204–220; Robert E. Park, "Assimilation, Social," in Edwin R. A. Seligman and Alvin Johnson (eds.), *Encyclopedia of the Social Sciences*, Vol. I–II (New York: Macmillan, 1930), pp. 281–283.

[27] Gordon, *op. cit.*, p. 89.

[28] W. D. Borrie, *The Cultural Integration of Immigrants* (Paris: UNESCO, 1959), p. 94.

[29] William Foot Whyte, *Street Corner Society, The Social Structure of an Italian Slum* (Chicago: University of Chicago Press, 1943); Herbert J. Gans, *The Urban Villagers, Group and Class in the Life of Italian Americans* (New York: Free Press, 1962).

[30] Ruby Jo Reeves Kennedy, "Single or Triple Melting Pot? Intermarriage in New Haven, 1870–1950," *American Journal of Sociology*, 58, no. 1 (July 1952), 56–59.

[31] D. C. Useem and Ruth H. Useem, "Minority Group Pattern in Prairie Society," *American Journal of Sociology*, 50 (June 1945), 377–385.

[32] S. N. Eisenstadt, *The Absorption of Immigrants* (London: Routledge and Kegan Paul, 1954).

[33] Borrie, *op. cit.*, p. 93.

[34] William Bernard in Borrie, *op. cit.*, p. 94.

[35] For further discussion of this point, see S. Lieberson, "A Societal Theory of Race and Ethnic Relations," *American Sociological Review*, Vol. 26 (December 1961).

[36] Roy Jenkins P.C.M.P. (Privy Councillor, Member of Parliament), in *Report of a Conference on Racial Equality in Employment* (London: National Committee for Commonwealth Immigrants, 1967), p. 8. Reproduced by permission.

[37] Mary Grigg, *The White Question* (London: Secker and Warburg, 1967), pp. 180–181.

[38] See Sheila Patterson, *Dark Strangers* (London: Tavistock, 1963), pp. 6–9; Sheila Patterson, *Immigrants in Industry* (London: Oxford University Press, 1968), pp. 3–9.

[39] Dipak Nandy, "Those Unrealistic Aspirations," *Race Today* (May 1969).

[40] Patterson, *Dark Strangers, op. cit.,* pp. 6–7.

[41] *Ibid.,* p. 7.

[42] Lloyd Warner and Leo Srole, *The Social Systems of American Ethnic Groups* (New Haven: Yale University Press, 1945), p. 286, quoted in P. I. Rose, *They and We, Racial and Ethnic Relations in the United States* (New York: Random House, 1964), p. 12.

[43] See *Report on Racial Discrimination* (London: Political and Economic Planning, April 1967), pp. 32–33.

[44] Many theories assume that there is a "cycle" of race relations that moves through phases of initial contact to a stage of assimilation. See Berry, *op. cit.,* pp. 129–134.

[45] W. J. Cahnman and A. Boskoff (eds.), *Sociology and History* (New York: Free Press, 1964), p. 569.

[46] For a stimulating approach to differential intergroup relations and the important distinction between migrant superordination and native (host) subordination as opposed to migrant subordination and native superordination, see Lieberson, *op. cit.,* pp. 902–910.

Chapter 2 ◉ Colored Immigration to Britain

PERSPECTIVES ON MIGRATION

In the past decade immigration has become accepted as "a problem" in Britain. The questions raised about immigrants in specific situations often have an apparent simplicity. Why have the immigrants come? How long do they plan to stay? How many more will arrive and how many can be taken? The answers may be simple assertions of selected facts or particular beliefs. In themselves, these answers are of interest because they indicate how certain groups within the receiving society have evaluated and given meaning to a particular migration. Some of these evaluations will be discussed in this and the following chapters.

For those who wish to understand the processes involved in migration, simple assertions are inadequate. The assumption that individual motivation can satisfactorily account for the migration of particular groups ignores the social constraints on individual decision making, neglecting the pressures within the native environment and failing to examine the situation within the receiving society. Each individual has reasons for migrating or staying home, but to interpret migration processes on a personal basis is to treat the individual as an entity autonomous from social forces and thus fail to confront the structure and process of migration. For example, in assessing the migration of West Indians to Britain, an account of individual motives and experiences is sociologically useful, when this level of analysis is seen in the context of the overall relationships that have developed over time, and continue to develop, between the West Indies and Britain. The migration is not only the result of individual motivation or immediate elements within the present situation.

Immigration and emigration have been constant features in British society. The recent immigration of colored people is only one phase. A variety of factors have been involved at different times, each of which can be studied in terms of its effects on the patterns of social relations within Britain and the interrelation with social processes at work in other societies. To single out one phase in the total process inevitably does less than justice to the intricacies of the interrelationships between the institutions of one society and those of the other societies from which or to which people migrate. If we examine only one end of the migration process, for instance, the arrival in Britain of colored immigrants, many important factors predisposing certain groups to emigrate are left out. These factors, nevertheless, influence behavior in the new environment. In practical terms, the permanent or temporary nature of migration is, to some extent, dependent on the circumstances the immigrant leaves and the ones he enters. When migration statistics are used to distinguish between different types of migration, several problems arise. The distinction between travelers or visitors and permanent immigrants, for example, is frequently based on an arbitrary, sometimes statutory, time limit. Moreover, the distinction between internal and international migration assumes a significance that is not necessarily much use in explaining the causes and consequences of migration. In sociological inquiries, statistical data, collected for administrative purposes, must be handled with care when the data presuppose a relevance of distinctions that are problematic in sociological analysis. The difficulties involved are highlighted by the case of a woman from British Honduras who wished to visit her two daughters and grandchildren settled in Britain. By asking to be allowed to stay indefinitely the woman came into the permanent category although this was not her intention. Her treatment by immigration officials was affected by the categorization as the following explanation of one of her daughters indicates:

> . . . my mother is now meditating on the subtle distinction between "indefinitely," the time for which she asked to be

allowed to stay here, and "permanently," which British officials, including the Home Secretary, have declared a synonymous word, and what she really meant. My mother thinks, and so do I, these words are very different; for none of us lives in the world permanently, but all of us most indefinitely.[1]

Many analyses of migration start with the assumption that man is normally stable and the analyses then proceed to explain why people migrate.[2] This view has been criticized by William Petersen who remarks, "Like most psychological universals, this one can be matched by its opposite: man migrates because of wanderlust. And like all such universals, these cannot explain differential behaviour: if all men are sedentary [or migratory] 'by nature,' why do some migrate and some not?"[3] No general theory of migration has yet been developed. Most studies involve some notion of a push-pull complex and a broad distinction between forced and voluntary migration. In critically reviewing some of the predominant assumptions in work on internal and international migration, Petersen presents a typology which seeks to avoid some of the common confusions about migration and to clarify some of the problems that need investigation. He distinguishes five types of migration of general relevance; primitive, forced, impelled, free, and mass. These types are differentiated in relation to both the causes of migration and the likely consequences of migration.[4]

Primitive migration, which includes the wandering of peoples, the ranging of nomads and gatherers, and the flight from the land, is due to ecological push and controls "usually geographical, but sometimes social." The "flight from the land" category is ambiguous in terms of causes and the other categories are not relevant to the situation under examination. Only a few colored immigrants can be properly included in the forced category—some Kenyan Asians and others, individuals of Indo-Pakistan origin, for instance. Certain groups of white migrants, including the displaced persons of largely eastern European origin, who settled in Britain during the immediate postwar period, would be classified likewise. The last three, impelled, free, and mass migration, are of particular interest to the present discussion.

Petersen distinguishes impelled migration from forced migration. He feels that in the case of impelled migration, migrants, when confronted with state pressures, have some power of decision as to whether they leave or not. Such pressures may be negative, that is, simply moving people from a certain territory; on the other hand, they may be positive, seeking removal of inhabitants in order to induce them to provide labor power elsewhere.* The partition of India and the creation of the State of Pakistan in 1947 led to large movements of population, taking place under governmental arrangements and as a result of violence or the threat of violence. It is an example of impelled negative migration that eventually led, in some instances, to further migration to the United Kingdom. Other cases of impelled migration are less clear. How far, for instance, do advertized inducements to move, accompanied by restrictions in opportunities to maintain a certain level of livelihood at home, constitute impelled migration? An example, such as the activities of London Transport, along with West Indian governments in the early 1950s, is a case in point. Instances of impelled migration are frequently difficult to document while they are in process or immediately afterward. The migration to Britain of Indians, West Indians, and Pakistanis is no exception. It tends to be treated officially as though it were "free" migration. In many instances, this may well be; however, some features of this migration would warrant consideration under the impelled category.†

Petersen claims that "free migration is always rather small, for individuals strongly motivated to seek novelty or improve-

---

* Petersen calls these negative or positive pressures conservative or innovative migration, respectively. In the former, the geographical location, only, is changed; in the latter, new patterns of behavior can be expected to develop.

† One example that appears to contain elements of impelled migration is the migration to Britain of large numbers of Kashmiris from Azad Kashmir who came in a matter of months, working and living largely in one area and one industry. The forces involved are reputed to be not only the labor power sought by employers but also an agreement at governmental levels. Such an explanation that is strongly held by many migrants may have no basis in fact. But a satisfactory explanation of how so many rural illiterate Kashmiris decided to emigrate at one point in time must await further evidence.[5]

ment are not commonplace."[6] He points to the importance
such migration not in terms of numbers but in terms of setting
a pattern and providing an example that can, in some circumstances, develop into a mass or collective emigration. During
the nineteenth century the movement from Northern Europe to
the United States illustrated the initial pioneer emigration of
small numbers of free migrants followed by group migration
and, after the 1860s, by mass migration. In the first stage, individual motivation and characteristics are significant in explaining the movement, but gradually, as a pattern of emigration is created, individual attitudes become less important in
explanatory terms. Much of the recent emigration to Britain
from the colored Commonwealth fits the pattern of mass migration. Once the possibility of movement to Britain was established, the individual motivations became less relevant in
explaining the migration process than the social forces in Britain and the home environment. Before considering some of the
particular factors involved in this process, the position of the
colored population in Britain, previous to this migration, will be
described briefly.

THE SITUATION BEFORE 1950

Until the end of World War II in 1945, the numbers of colored
residents in Britain were extremely small. They consisted of
seamen, servicemen, workers brought over to fill labor shortages
in the two wars, peddlers, as well as students, businessmen, and
professionals. The seamen had become a regular feature of seaport life during the nineteenth century. They lived in the dock
areas of Liverpool, Cardiff, Bristol, London, and the Northeast.
Frequently intermarrying and settling in Britain, they became
part of local communities. Their integration was to the life of
a seaport; the seamen were frequently absent and largely segregated, for their lives were governed by the rhythm of seagoing
communities. In this sense, they shared with all seamen a structurally marginal position. Studies of these communities have
formed the basis of much of the work on race relations in
Britain.[7] Of the Pakistani, ex-seaman Hamza Alavi comments:

. . . [they] were men who had "seen the world." They were detribalised. They adopted British customs more readily . . . . Taking alcoholic drink perhaps represents the greatest extreme for the Pakistani worker in the abandonment of traditional values . . . . Some of the early settlers married local women and seem to have adapted themselves to local life without too much difficulty.[8]

And likewise of Indians, Rashmi Desai says, "They usually live with non-Indian women and in the colored settlements in the ports. They have no contact with the new immigrants."[9] Negro and Arab seamen settled in the dock area of Cardiff, Butetown, toward the end of the nineteenth century. By the mid-forties the community had reached about 7,000 and included other colored immigrants who arrived mainly during the two wars. Intermarriage with the white community took place and the succeeding generations, while still largely confined to the same geographical area, took industrial jobs and came to regard themselves as Welsh, despite a large and growing Muslim section. According to a recent study, contact between the colored community and the new immigrants is small and competition for industrial jobs, in a city where 70 percent of the employment is distributive, professional, and clerical leads the established colored community to discourage more colored immigration.[10]

In addition to the seamen, later joined by other ex-servicemen and munitions workers, there were also students, business and professional men. Since the beginning of British rule in India, Indians often came to Britain to be educated at public schools and the older universities.* Most returned home, but some remained to practice law or medicine or become politicians in the British House of Commons. The professional groups did not form separate geographical or social units and many became anglicized, practicing in white communities. Likewise, the businessmen were frequently linked with white companies that had

---

* Pakistanis are of course included in the term "Indians" here. Public schools are private schools, independent of the State. They charge high fees and provide an exclusive form of education for about 2 percent of the children of school age.

interests in India but, unlike the peddlers, many of whom were long resident in Britain, the businessmen did not operate from communities of Indians who kept close ties with India. In 1949 it was estimated that there were 5,000 Indians who had been in Britain for a fairly lengthy period.[11] Of these, 500 were seamen settling before World War II and between 3,000 and 4,000 were peddlers and their dependents. The remainder included the professional and business groups.

West Indian servicemen and war workers had come during the two wars, particularly during World War II, and about one-third of these were still in Britain in the early 1950s. They either chose to be demobilized in Britain or returned, soon after demobilization in the home islands. War gratuities were used to pay fares or buy houses, and, in some cases, helped toward making higher education possible for West Indian ex-servicemen. In addition, the gratuities enabled Pakistani ex-servicemen to establish such businesses as restaurants, grocery shops, and lodging houses.

The colored population of Britain in 1950 included students who stayed only long enough to complete their education and a variety of groups that had settled at different times for different reasons. Patterns of social relationships developed in accordance with the occupational level, the socioeconomic characteristics of the areas in which the groups lived, the degree to which intermarriage was practiced, and the degree to which separate religious observances, particularly those of Islam, were maintained. Segregation into largely colored communities became an established pattern for some groups, their children and grandchildren included, while other groups were found in entirely white districts. Many became like the majority of the population in speech, dress, ways of living, and expectations for themselves and their children. The degree of acceptance was never entirely a matter of color; socioeconomic factors played a large part. However, the fact that color was and could be used as a means of social differentiation was shown not only by the evidence of segregation prior to 1950 but also by the developments since that time. Colored Welsh and English people who have never been outside the United Kingdom now find themselves categorized socially and treated as immigrants.

IMMIGRATION AFTER 1950

Some Predisposing Factors

Migration from the West Indies, India, and Pakistan is not a new phenomenon. The obvious "push" factors toward migration are demographic and economic. From the overpopulated and underemployed islands of the West Indies, migrants have gone to the United States, Panama, Cuba, and Puerto Rico, as well as Canada. Between 1881 and 1953 there was a net outward movement from Jamaica, alone, of over 150,000. In Barbados, where the population density in 1954 was 1,380 per square mile, government assisted schemes of emigration exist, but, in the other islands, the emigration has been privately undertaken and organized. As the United States government tightened restrictions on the immigration of West Indians, culminating in the McCarren Act of 1952, the natural inlet for emigrants was virtually closed.* Therefore, migrants increasingly came to Britain. (See Map 3 in Appendix.) Similarly India (including Pakistan before 1947) exported people to areas where labor was needed. Between 1834 and 1937 the total emigration from India had been estimated at slightly more than 30 million, but, of these, 24 million returned. Therefore, during the century net emigration was 6 million.[12] Much of this movement was indentured or contract labor and only within the British Empire as it then was.† East and South Africa, the West Indies, and Southeast Asia, particularly Malaya and parts of Borneo, have considerable settlements of Indians, recruited for specific work, who remained and whose descendants became skilled workers, white collar employees, as well as tradesmen, and professionals. Political and social changes closed many of these inlets, although the demographic, economic, and, in some cases, political developments in India and Pakistan continued and increased

---

* West Indians are now recruited to work in farm employment in the United States for short contracts only. Several thousand such workers are recruited each year under the supervision of an official government agency.
† This is a clear example of impelled migration.

in intensity as factors pushing toward emigration. After 1955 migrants from India and Pakistan began to enter Britain in increasing numbers. (See Maps 1 and 2 in Appendix.) They came from the Punjab, particularly the districts of Jullundar and Hoshiarpur, and from the central and southern parts of Gujerat where there is great pressure on the land and widespread unemployment. Emigration has become a traditional solution. From the West Punjab in Pakistan, the northwest frontier area, the Mirpur district of Kashmir, the Sylhet district, and coastal areas in East Pakistan, the emigration was, in some cases, traditional and, in other cases, augmented by political pressures and disputes leading to further economic dislocation.[13]

Emigration from certain areas creates acute problems. There is not a simple gain as a result of reduction in unemployment and receipt of remittances from those who have left. The debit side is twofold. First, there is a depletion of certain age groups —those most able to contribute to the economy and those who must be replaced from an already short supply of skilled labor. Secondly, when dependent children, old people, and even wives in many instances are left behind, social problems are created. R. B. Davison describes this situation in the West Indies as "appalling."[14] In India and Pakistan the family structure may be more able to absorb the problems caused by emigration; however, there, too, the social consequences of emigration cannot be ignored. The changes in the control of immigration to Britain that came into effect in 1965, giving preference to skilled and professionally qualified immigrants and tightening the regulations for dependents, exacerbated the dual problems. (For a discussion of the consequences of these regulations, see pp. 49–54.)

The factors already mentioned may be regarded as predisposing conditions for emigration, but, as the evidence from the West Indian territories show, there is no direct relation between population density and the volume of emigration. In the case of economic conditions the relationship is a more direct one. (See Tables 1A and 2A in Appendix.) Where emigrants go is largely determined by the policies of the external governments. Whether they go at all and how many leave, in the case of migrants who are moving mainly for economic reasons, seems to depend less on the conditions at home than on the migrant's assessment of the demand for labor in the country to which they are going. William Petersen elaborates as follows:

> Economic hardship, for example, can be termed a "cause" of emigration only if there is a positive correlation between hardship, however defined and the propensity to emigrate. Often the relation has been an inverse one . . . the mass migration from Europe in modern times developed together with a marked *rise* in the European standard of living. As has been shown by several studies, the correlation was rather with the business cycle in the receiving country, and even this relationship explains fluctuations in the emigration rate more than its absolute level.[15]

The same confusion of "causes" relates to religious and political factors. The evidence from nineteenth century Europe shows "that those who emigrated because of persecution tended to come from countries where there was less than elsewhere."[16] That is, when the emigrant had a choice of staying or leaving, he would take into consideration his chances of getting work elsewhere. Of course, there are always exceptions to this general thesis. In times of extreme persecution, such as the eastern European pogroms of the late nineteenth century, the exodus is largely explained in terms of fleeing from persecution rather than seeking opportunities in the receiving countries. The movement of dependents, wives, children, and old people is subject to the same conditions, though indirectly.[17]

Although the immigration to Britain in the early fifties was largely privately organized by the migrants or their families and friends, the situation changed toward the middle of the 1950s. In 1953 only three ships, making five sailings a year, were involved in carrying migrants from the West Indies to Britain. By 1955 thirteen ships, making forty sailings a year, were involved and the number of passengers per ship had increased. Later, charter flights were also added as a means of bringing West Indians to Britain. By the early 1960s charter flights became the most important means of transport. Travel agents, shipping lines, and air companies became actively involved in the migration. Offers of cheap fares and allegedly unscrupulous advertizing were used to induce immigrants. In India and Pakistan "agents" began to operate. By exaggerating the benefits of Britain and arranging passports and passages, they persuaded and facilitated the migration of people from the villages. The influence of these activities on the volume of migration is difficult to assess. Although the earlier Pakistani and Indian migrants usually had relatives in Britain, the later ones frequently knew only the people from the same village with whom they had traveled. Many governments played very little part in the organization of migration either positively or negatively. Barbados assisted emigrants, Jamaica discouraged them, and after 1958 Pakistan took strong measures to control emigration. In view of the previously discussed typology of migration, the recent migration to Britain can be characterized as mass migration with elements of impelled migration playing an important part. The migration to Britain is one phase of a longstanding movement and the volume and composition are the outcome of particular elements within a situation in which legislation in Britain has become increasingly significant.

The Campaign for Control

The campaign to control immigration from the Commonwealth gathered momentum in the late 1950s. In the middle of the fifties the campaign in Parliament "was confined to a handful of Conservative Members. It was, however, pursued with tenacity from 1955 onwards. . . . Despite the discouraging response from the Government the campaign continued relentlessly and the Press began to give some publicity to the matter. The problem began to feature also in television programmes."[18] Two events brought the question of colored-white relations into sharp focus. Considerable violence took place in Nottingham and London during the summer of 1958. Attacks on colored people and their homes brought counterattacks; as tension mounted, groups of whites, in some cases organized, threatened and manhandled colored passers-by to such an extent that the police advised colored people to keep off the streets, provided protection for those returning home from work at night, and increased policing of the areas. In the Notting Hill area of

London and certain adjacent areas, the tension and disturbances continued for several days.[19] Nine white youths, armed with a variety of weapons, had systematically toured the area seeking colored men on their own or in twos, and attacking them. The youths were arrested and each was subsequently sentenced to four years imprisonment. This case became famous as a result of the judgment of Justice Salmon who gave the following verdict:

> . . . Everyone, irrespective of the colour of their skin, is entitled to walk through our streets in peace, with their heads erect, and free from fear. That is a right which these courts will always unfailingly uphold.
>
> As far as the law is concerned you are entitled to think what you like, however foul your thoughts; to feel what you like, however brutal and debased your emotions; to say what you like providing you do not infringe the rights of others or imperil the Queen's peace, but once you translate your dark thoughts and brutal feelings into savage acts such as these the law will be swift to punish you, the guilty and protect your victims.[20]

In May 1959 a young West Indian carpenter was murdered in North Kensington as he walked home alone from a hospital. Eye witnesses alleged that he was attacked by five or six white youths. The murder revived the fears and tensions and the publicity of the previous summer. Public discussion following both events was, in many cases, sensational and sentimental, but attempts were also made to find the causes and to explain the situation. These attempts focused on the social problems of decaying urban areas; on the activities of the "white lunatic fringe," commonly thought to be poorly educated, of low intelligence, and socially and economically insecure; and on the "color problem," aggravated by increased numbers of colored people, especially "undesirable" colored immigrants. The public shock and disapproval of the events reflected what was widely viewed as the traditional British attitude toward manifestations of racialism.

The three major political parties rejected control of Commonwealth immigration and refuted the allegations of sick, lazy, and criminal immigrants invading Britain. The Labour party's official view, for instance, stated, "We are firmly convinced that any form of British legislation limiting Commonwealth immigration into this country would be disastrous to our status in the Commonwealth and to the confidence of Commonwealth peoples."[21] This view was repeated even more firmly during a debate on immigration control in December 1958, when the Labour party argued against restriction on principle and rejected deportation of criminals. It maintained that any criminal was to be treated in the same way, whatever his race, color, or creed. The Conservative government was also opposed to general control of immigration; but, it did consider the possibility of deporting criminals and the possibility of agreements with Commonwealth governments on the question of immigration.

The ugliness of racialism, though condemned, was open to differing interpretations and the "solutions" offered were not solely of the liberal kind. One interpretation of the events of 1958 and 1959 was that colored people created a race problem and the solution was to keep them out, either altogether or severely reduce their numbers. After the Notting Hill disturbances, the small minority of Conservative members advocating restriction were joined by a few Labour members. "The Government must introduce legislation quickly to end the tremendous influx of coloured people from the Commonwealth . . . . For years white people have been tolerant. Now their tempers are up," commented George Rogers, the Labour member of Parliament for the Notting Hill area.[22] Although this minority view was shunned by "responsible" opinion in Parliament, by the press, and by church and trade union leaders, it was less than four years later that legislation to control immigration to Britain from the Commonwealth was passed. The Labour party continued to reject control of Commonwealth immigration and opposed the bill in 1962 on social and economic grounds, as well as principle. Many Conservatives spoke against the bill and the Liberals opposed it outright. Extremist political groups such as the Union movement, the League of Empire Loyalists, the National Labour party,* and the White Defense League systematically exploited the arrival of colored people to promote racial hatred on the basis of racial fears. These groups were small and their activities considered marginal in the mainstream of political and social life. Some groups put up candidates for elections both locally and nationally, but they specialized in propaganda activities, often of a virulent racialist nature. Some felt the immigration of colored people to Britain was due to the Jewish influence; they associated color with infectious diseases, including leprosy, alleged that colored people lived off state benefits, and, above all, were a threat to race purity—mongrelization was a favorite theme. Anxiety about such propaganda and its consequences was expressed and many times attempts were made in the House of Commons to introduce legislation making the dissemination of such propaganda a criminal offence. For instance, seven Labour members of Parliament brought in a bill which had its first reading in February 1960 to make it illegal "to insult publicly or to conspire to insult publicly any person or persons because of their race or religion," but the bill was not successful, as it was argued that prosecution under existing common law was sufficient to deal with the problem. The general view was to treat such propaganda activities as unrepresentative, "un-British," and therefore of no consequence.

The majority of those campaigning for immigration control disassociated themselves from the extreme right-wing groups in two ways. First, they went to some lengths to explain that favoring control was not motivated by anti-color feelings and was not intended to apply to colored people alone. Although arguments similar to those of the extremists were used, they were usually expressed in more acceptable language. They used the situation of ambiguity about racial prejudice existing in Britain—on the one hand, deploring it, on the other, exploiting what were believed to be the inevitable results. For instance, in December 1958, Martin Lindsay, seconding a motion

---

* Formed in May 1958 by a small group who left the Empire Loyalists in order to fight both communism and liberal democracy. The National Labour party is both anti-Semitic and anti-colored.

on control of immigration, irrespective of race, color, or creed, said, "I could not find any excuses whatever for anyone who believed in a colour bar in any community where black and white have to co-exist. That, however, is altogether different from changing the nature of a community."[24] At the local level this disassociation from anticolor was not always achieved. A Birmingham city councillor writing to a local paper maintained, "Birmingham needs protection from coloured marauders. I would that there were 500 of us grouped together with one ideal: to stop the uncontrolled influx of coloured immigrants."[25] A short time later the councillor became the first chairman of the Birmingham Immigration Control Association. Two other associations were formed in the Birmingham area within a few months.

Secondly, none of these associations had any formal organizational links with the extreme right-wing groups. They campaigned on the single issue of immigration, using social and economic arguments against colored immigrants. Their main arguments were the following: Britain could not afford the luxury of colored immigrants who, if they did not create the housing problem, worsened it; immigrant demands on the medical and other social services, to which it was alleged they had not contributed, were too high; in addition, children of colored immigrants posed costly problems in terms of education, and, moreover, their different habits and customs made them unacceptable to so many who did not want a multiracial Britain. The associations acted as pressure groups on the local Conservative and Labour organizations, the local members of Parliament, the trade union branches, and the white electorate. They succeeded in making colored immigration a political issue— few members of Parliament or local party officials and workers found the resources to prevent this and some actively welcomed it. With the help of some local newspapers who printed letters supporting control on the above grounds and gave coverage to anti-immigrant meetings, an active, if small, minority produced an atmosphere in which the solution to the housing, education, or any other social and economic problem was to be found in "keeping out the blacks." Local activists appeared in other areas who, although they did not succeed in forming associations before the 1962 Act, have, in some cases, particularly in London and the Midlands, done so since. The associations have not established anything more than uneasy, often temporary, links with local party organizations, but their success lies not in taking over any party groupings but through challenging the acceptability of a multiracial Britain and through defining color as a problem linked with existing problems. There are now few local or national politicians who cannot at least be embarrassed by the color question and a majority who find it expedient to support control and to express concern over immigrant problems.

The major change in policy made by the government in 1962 and the confirmation and extension of the new policy by subsequent governments has been part of a broader social process in Britain of interpreting race relations as race problems and equating these with the presence of colored people. It was a short, if logically erroneous, step to assume that colored people created social and economic problems and were responsible for the increase in racialism. Such interpretations make it possible for people without prejudice themselves to act, because they fear the consequences that they believe will inevitably flow from the prejudices of others. The "solution" then seems to lie in control of the entry of immigrants and in education to bring about integration. The experience of the campaign for control and the dwindling opposition to such a policy in the years since 1962 demonstrate how ideas, expressly repudiated by the majority, can, through the selection, presentation, and constant repetition of "inexorable social facts," come to be officially adopted and legitimated in practice. Racialism is exacerbated not only by highly prejudiced fringe groups but also by activities stemming from the fears of the well-intentioned.*

---

* In February 1968 the Commonwealth Immigrants Act 1968 was passed. This measure, introduced and passed in a matter of days, involved breaking a pledge given to Kenyan Asians at the time of Kenya's independence and making the right of entry of British citizens conditional. Government spokesmen denied that the legislation was racialist, but it was felt by many that if the legislation was not radical in intent, it was in its consequences. It controls the entry of colored British subjects and not white British subjects. Those immediately affected were Kenyan Asians who did not possess Kenyan but British citizenship. Despite widespread criticism, the bill was passed on a free

The Volume and Social Composition of Immigration

As more statistical evidence has become available about the numbers, rate, and proportion of colored immigration in relation to other immigrants and the total population of the United Kingdom, many of the estimates used earlier are shown to have been greatly exaggerated. During 1960 and 1961 few reliable figures were available and highly emotive terms like "flood," "invasion," and "influx" were used to describe colored immigration. One observer claimed that "it was the gravest social crisis since the industrial revolution."[27] At the present time, national statistics relate not to color or race, but to place of birth, so, for many purposes, the statistics cannot be regarded as a satisfactory measure; however, they do provide a general indication of the size and rate of immigration from the colored Commonwealth. At the end of 1966, out of a population in Great Britain of over 55 million, about 1 million residents were thought to be colored immigrants from the Commonwealth or to have one or both parents who had emigrated from the Commonwealth, which is less than 2 percent of the total population.[28] The claim that Britain was becoming overcrowded because of the "flood" of immigrants ignored the figures on net migration which showed that in six of the twelve years, between 1953 and 1964, emigration exceeded immigration. The figures in Table 1 include migration to and from all

Table 1.   *Net Migration Balance, United Kingdom*

1953	−74,000	1959	+44,000
1954	−32,000	1960	+82,000
1955	−10,000	1961	+170,000
1956	−17,000	1962	+136,000
1957	−72,000	1963	+10,000
1958	+45,000	1964	−17,000

SOURCE: General Register Office, "Overseas Migration Board Statistics," Cmnd. 2861 (London:H.M.S.O., December 1965). Reproduced by permission.

vote and many who had opposed the 1962 Act, including the ministers of the Labour government, supported the legislation by their votes and their silence.[26]

countries, Commonwealth and non-Commonwealth. One cause
of the gain in 1958 was the drop in the numbers of those emi-
grating. "Between 1948 and 1957, emigration fluctuated
[roughly] between 100,000 and 140,000 per annum. But in
1958 it dropped to 93,796 and by 1961 it had dropped to 78,593
. . . . Immigration, on the other hand, was in 1957 and 1958
the lowest for years."[29]

The alarm at colored immigration and the use of exaggerated estimates of numbers may have been due, to some extent,
to comparison with the previous situation. In 1951 some 170,-
000 people in England and Wales had been born in Asian,
African, and the Caribbean Commonwealth countries; moreover this figure included both the white and the colored. By
1961 there were 446,000. The colored Commonwealth group
represented only 1 in 5 of all immigrants (see Table 2).

Table 2. Immigrants by Place of Birth, 1961

PLACE OF BIRTH	ENGLAND AND WALES (IN PERCENT) 1961
Ireland	38
Foreign	33
Colored Commonwealth	20
Other Commonwealth	9
Total	100

SOURCE: Kenneth Leech, "Migration and the British
Population, 1955–1962," *Race*, 7, 4, published for the
Institute of Race Relations (London: Oxford University Press, © Institute of Race Relations, April
1966), 405. Reproduced by permission.

The rate of growth, however, was the highest of any group
between 1951 and 1961 (see Table 3).

Within the increase of 276,000 between 1951 and 1961
three groups were given special attention. They were the people
coming from the West Indies, India, and Pakistan. (See Tables
3A and 4A in Appendix for statistics relating to their migration to Britain.) From each of these countries it was assumed
that the large numbers were accelerating at a steady rate. The

Table 3.   Changes in the Composition of the Population in
Terms of Birthplace, 1951–1961

Place of Birth	ENGLAND AND WALES CHANGES 1951–61	
	Number	In Percent
Great Britain	+1,839	+4
Ireland	+243	+39
Colored Commonwealth	+276	+162
Other Commonwealth	+64	+43
Foreign	+114	+18

SOURCE: Ruth Glass and John Westergaard, *London's Housing Needs* (London: Centre for Urban Studies, 1965), p. 32, Table 10b. Reproduced by permission.

credibility of such observations that the West Indians could ". . . in less than half a century outnumber us English, and with one man one vote . . . take over this country . . .,"[30] though challenged, was not dismissed as effectively as the figures involved would suggest. Many argued that without governmental controls increasing numbers would arrive; others claimed that the threats of controls were distorting migration trends.[31] The 1960, 1961, and early 1962 figures continued to be used by both sides in the argument about controls for some years after 1962, when the rate declined by comparison to these years. In an examination of the trends of migration before and after controls were imposed, Ceri Peach stresses the relation between the economic situation in Britain, particularly the employment situation, and the inflow of migrants. He concludes:

The real reason for the decline in the net inflow of migrants is two-fold. Firstly, the decline in the demand for labour decreased the number of arrivals. Secondly, the strain of the large number of arrivals at a time of low demand for labour before the enforcement of the Act gave rise to a very high rate of return—a backwash—which became evident after June 1962. The view that the Commonwealth Immigrants Act produced a major decline in the *net inflow* of Commonwealth immigrants is acceptable only if the view is also accepted that it produced a major rise before it came into effect. The effect of the Act after 1 July, 1962 was more apparent than real.[32]

The control of immigration of Commonwealth citizens into Britain was first implemented in 1962 and subsequent amendments in administrative practices and the Immigrants' Act of 1968 have tightened the control even more. Control of immigration is relevant in its effects on the total volume and the social composition of immigration and, more generally, in terms of race relations, particularly in view of the public debates on immigration that accompanied its introduction and each annual renewal.

Cedric Thornberry comments:

The Commonwealth Immigrants Act, regulating the position of Commonwealth citizens, has often been described as liberal. But it is only against the background of the draconian aliens' régime that such comment is meaningful. Had not the possibility of that comparison existed, several of the more obnoxious provisions of the Commonwealth Immigrants' Act could not have passed into law.*[33]

Before the Commonwealth Immigrants' Act of 1962, entry to Britain for citizens of her former Empire, now largely members of independent nations in the Commonwealth, was a right. There had been no deliberate act of policy embodied in any law, but it was an established custom. "It is simply a fact which we have taken for granted from the earliest days in which our forebears ventured forth across the seas."[34] This right was removed in 1962 and further restrictions imposed three years later. Certain categories are exempt from control. For those subject to control, an elaborate system of categories, each subject to varying rules of entry, has produced allegations of "evasions" on the one hand and of "arbitrary and capricious behavior" on the other. (The main categories and the system of admission are set out in Appendix III.) The annual debate

---

* It is now the policy of the Conservative party to amalgamate the legislation on Commonwealth and alien immigration and put the immigrants on the same footing in relation to entry, residence restrictions, and departure regulations.

in Parliament to renew control over immigration from other parts of the Commonwealth keeps the subject in the public eye. This affords an opportunity to indulge officially in chauvinism and racialism, to attribute the need for control to the criminal tendencies and health risks involved in immigration and to the social problems of housing, education, and the like created by immigrants. Refutations, carefully and closely argued, are also put forth; however, because immigration is legally restricted, there must be good reason for immigration control and the advantage is now with those who wish to tighten the restriction even further or who simply want to keep out colored people. In this sense, the legislation controlling entry of Commonwealth citizens does not improve the prospects for good relations between colored and white citizens in Britain. In November 1964 Aubrey Jones, a former Conservative minister, argued, "What has worried me . . . is the suggestion that if we reduce the numbers of immigrants, then automatically the immigrant population already here will be assimilated and everything will come right. I believe that this is the wrong way to look at the problem."[35]

The administration of control creates additional problems and the issues are usually discussed in colored-white terms. Since 1965, Commonwealth citizens who wish to work in Britain are admitted only if they have a specific job awaiting them or possess special qualifications and training, such as doctors, dentists, nurses, teachers, and scientists. Between 1962 and 1965 a limited number of vouchers were available for those who did not possess particular skills or a specific job but wanted to work in Britain. In September 1965 David Pitt said that it was not only a problem of color prejudice that confronted Britain but social prejudice as well: it was not right for doctors to enter the country on special vouchers when manual laborers were kept out.[36] It is argued that the control does not give preference to white immigrants and discriminate against colored people. When scarce high level professional or trained people are concerned, this is probably true. Nonetheless, for would-be immigrants who wish to work in lower status occupations, discrimination appears to be operated on a color basis.

A letter to the London *Times* outlines the difficulties that confronted a prospective employer who was trying to arrange for a Trinidadian nurse with experience and first class references to look after his children. Describing what he called "the fratricidal fury of previous and present administrations against Commonwealth citizens," he went on to say:

> As soon as I telephoned the Ministry of Labour to find out the procedure for obtaining a work permit, the machinery of dissuasion swung into ponderous operation. I was advised that as there was such a long delay before any person from the Commonwealth could be admitted notwithstanding job and accommodation being available, it would be advisable to look for a German or Austrian or other European help as they could be given a permit immediately if there was a post available for them.[37]

The number of Commonwealth citizens entering with work vouchers has been reduced considerably while the exception, made in the case of the Irish and the continued entry of workers from Europe, makes it difficult to refute the contention that the legislation is used to keep out Commonwealth and particularly colored Commonwealth citizens. During 1965 and 1966, of those admitted from the Commonwealth with Ministry of Labour vouchers, 10,827 came from Africa, Asia, and the Caribbean.[38] Of the 66,054 foreign workers given permission to work during 1966, 11,217 were already in this country as visitors (see Table 4).[39]

DEPENDENT RELATIVES. By far the largest group of Commonwealth citizens wishing to settle in the United Kingdom are dependents of immigrants already here. "The proportion of dependents to voucher-holders being admitted has gradually increased and in 1966 was nearly eight to one."[40] The administration of the regulations governing their entry has given rise to considerable disquiet within the immigrant communities in Britain. While the restrictions have been tightened, the allegations of discrimination and callous treatment at places of entry have grown. Since there is control and those seeking entry as dependents come into a variety of categories, delicate problems of who may or may not enter are bound to arise. A detached investigator can point to the minute proportion of the

Table 4.

YEAR	NUMBER OF FOREIGN WORKERS GRANTED PERMISSION TO WORK*	NUMBER OF COMMON-WEALTH CITIZENS ADMITTED ON WORK VOUCHERS†
1965	66,126	12,125
1966	66,054	5,141
1967	60,627	4,716
1968	62,267	4,353
1969	67,788	3,512
Totals	322,862	29,847

SOURCES: *Ministry of Labour Gazette,* 75, no. 3, p. 223 and 76, no. 3, p. 216 (London:H.M.S.O.); *Employment and Productivity Gazette,* 77, no. 3., p. 240 and 78, no. 3. Adapted by permission of Her Majesty's Stationery Office.

† Institute of Race Relations Facts Paper, *Colour and Immigration In The United Kingdom,* 1969, and Runnymeade Trust Industrial Unit.

total number of people refused entry (0.3 percent in 1966) and indicate that in "questioning people about their intentions and family circumstances, the Immigration Officers are only carrying out duties laid on them by Parliament,"[41] that the principles on which they exercise discretion are published by the Home Office, and that the conduct of immigration officers, in general, is courteous and fair within the established limits. From the standpoint of the migrant awaiting a relative and the immigrant seeking admission, the situation looks very different. The situation has a completely different meaning and importance for the individuals involved. Members of immigration bureaucracies, acting well within the obligations laid upon them, can create a situation of Kafka-like proportions for the client. How many immigrants would like a chance, along with the land surveyor in Kafka's *The Castle,* to say:

> . . . now again you're taking far too simple a view of the case. I'll enumerate for your benefit a few of the things that keep me here: the sacrifice I made in leaving my home, the long and difficult journey, the well-grounded hopes I built on my engagement here, my complete lack of means, the impossibility after this of finding some other

suitable job at home, and last but not least my fiancée, who lives here.[42]

The wife and children, under sixteen years, of an immigrant already here may be refused admission only if a deportation order is in force against them. In certain circumstances the age applying to children may be raised to eighteen or twenty-one. Parents over sixty and distressed relatives are also admitted under the same conditions as aliens. The most difficult problems that arise are mainly due to "verifying the relationship and age asserted by someone, seeking admission as a dependent relative, in whose country of origin there is no nation-wide system of recording birth, parentage and marriage."[43] Family details are checked by means of separate interviews of the would-be immigrants and the person with whom they claim a relationship; age is assessed by clinical assessment or x-ray examination of bones, although a crucial margin of error of two years is possible. Although the number refused entry is relatively small, the procedures designed to prevent illegal entry are humiliating, harassing, and, for some, particularly village women and young children, frightening.[44] Forged documents and false claims regarding age and relationship are made. Travel companies in India and Pakistan with agents in Europe are alleged to organize illegal entry and supply false documents.[45] The more intricate the restrictions, the more racketeers will flourish and the more indignities legal entrants will encounter. In terms of race relations in Britain, the result, on one side, is bitterness and cynicism and, on the other, stereotyped images of countless colored immigrants carrying forged documents, deceiving immigration officers, and landing illegally. The estimates are derived from the *difference* between the net overall gain in any one year and the total admitted for residence during the same period. This difference arises for many legitimate reasons and the two calculations are highly unlikely to balance at any one point in time. In 1963 and 1964 the statistical difference or "evasions" were greater for white Commonwealth than for colored Commonwealth citizens. Evasion proper, in the sense of illegal entry with false documents, statements, impersonations and the like, is not measurable.[46]

In relation to the totals for 1960, 1961, and the early part of

1962, there has been a reduction in the numbers arriving and any potential acceleration of the rate has been prevented. (See Appendix II.) The increasing preference given to skilled or specifically qualified people and the quota system, for those wishing to come to fill an existing job, have altered the social composition of immigration. The balance between the economically active immigrants and the ones coming as dependents of people already here has changed. Table 4A in Appendix II gives the breakdown for men, women, and children under sixteen years of age for the years after the 1962 Act. The earlier immigration in the case of all three groups, West Indians, Indians, and Pakistanis, followed a fairly common pattern of migration with a preponderance of young adults and a balance of males over females. Between 1955 and 1964 over 40 percent of the West Indian immigrants were women, while the immigration of Pakistanis was almost exclusively male. In 1961 there were less than 5,000 women in Britain who had been born in Pakistan, including both Pakistani citizens and citizens of the United Kingdom and the Colonies.* By 1963, 8 percent of the immigrants from Pakistan were women and in 1964, 19 percent were women. The proportion of women to men among immigrants from India falls between the other two groups and, by 1964, women made up about 27 percent of the Indians coming to Britain.[47] Asian women, unlike West Indian women, migrate mainly as dependents, along with, or more usually, following their husbands or other male kinsmen. In general, they are also less likely to take up employment outside the home after their arrival. The exception to this pattern are students or professionally qualified women who may come alone and work. Indian women are increasingly taking employment in unskilled or semiskilled jobs, but this group does not migrate independently of male relatives. The majority of West Indian women take employment after arrival, and though most migrate to join husbands or other relatives, some come independently. The increasing proportion of women and children in immigrant groups would be expected, even without controls,

---

* This figure, therefore, includes an unknown number of white women born in Pakistan.

because as men found jobs and living accommodations, they would be joined by their families. However, on the basis of the available statistics, it would not be justified to make categorical assertions about the relationship between the increasing balance of men and women and the stability or adjustment of the migrants. A priori, men with wives and children are likely to be more settled residents, but the threat of control and the ways in which immigration restrictions have worked are both significant factors in the change in social composition of the groups. Because of the uncertainty regarding entry regulations, wives and children came over earlier than they would have done otherwise; furthermore, the restriction of entry of those coming to work (mainly male) has been more stringent than the control of certain groups of dependents coming to join relatives who are already here. By keeping down the proportion of adult male entrants, the balancing of proportions has been accelerated.

DEPENDENT CHILDREN AND BIRTH RATES. An accurate proportion of children in immigrant groups is not known. Children under sixteen, arriving in Britain after 1962, are recorded and the figures appear in Appendix II, Table 4A. To these must be added figures for children born in Britain to colored immigrant parents. One estimate was that both these categories constituted about 75,000, or 30 percent, of the immigrant population in 1964. Fears are expressed, frequently in public, that Britain's colored population will increase at an alarming rate and the white population will be swamped. This anxiety rests on assumptions about the fertility of colored women immigrants and a particular interpretation of birth rates. Exaggerations, distortions, and misinterpretations have become so common because birth rates are used as ammunition in arguments for tighter controls on entry. The birth rates in the West Indies, India, and Pakistan are much higher, in some cases over double the average in the United Kingdom.[48] Among the immigrant groups in Britain, the estimated birth rate is higher than that of the English, twenty-five per 1,000 as against eighteen per 1,000. As a basis for deductions about future birth rates, these two facts have to be handled with caution. Population projections are not simple matters, even with a stable social situation. When they involve migratory groups in rapidly changing situations, they encompass a complex configuration of sociocultural variables.[49] Socialization in a traditional rural society with religious and cultural patterns that place a high value on childbearing is part of the cultural experience of many recent migrants to Britain. In India and, to a lesser extent, in Pakistan and the West Indies, population limitation and control is increasingly approved officially and is slowly gaining acceptance. However, even if we ignore the fact that many immigrants are aware of these conflicting values before they leave their home countries and even if we assume that their socialization has been of an extreme traditional nature, the sociocultural situation that they enter must also be examined. All the sociological evidence on birth rates demonstrates the relationship between the level of these rates and the structural conditions. Although this relationship and the social processes involved are not yet fully explained, there is no question that the general relationship between lower birth rates and industrialization is established, and there is no reason to assume that the immigrant groups in Britain will not follow a similar pattern. The fact that birth rates among these groups are already lower than rates in their countries of origin is some indication that this process has already begun. The fact that it remains higher than the average English rate is explained partly by the different age structures of the two communities. The immigrant groups consist largely of young adults and a particularly high proportion of women of childbearing age. Thus the ages of the groups, a factor frequently overlooked in discussions on the subject, account for the higher crude birth rate.

A study of the comparative fertility rates of four groups from different countries, now living in one part of Birmingham, contains interesting data on fertility patterns and on family planning knowledge and practices. Although only indications at this point, the results of this pilot inquiry show differences in the actual reproductive experiences among the women from the different groups and suggest the factors that may explain such variations.[50] In the sample, of the women who had been pregnant, the Irish had the highest average of pregnancies—4.5 percent compared to 3.8 percent for Indian/ Pakistani women, 3.3 percent for West Indian women, and 3.1 percent for English women. The average number of live births for the same groups within the sample were 3.5 percent for the Irish and Indian/Pakistani women, and 2.7 percent for the English and West Indian women. The information collected relating to family planning showed that the Indian/Pakistani group were the least informed, 68.1 percent compared to 92.8 percent of the Irish who were the most informed; 90.7 percent of the English and 87.5 percent of the West Indians fell between these limits. Although the Indian/Pakistani group were least informed of all the groups, the percentage that had knowledge of family planning was remarkably high. It does not fit the popular stereotype of Indian and Pakistani couples who, because of their largely rural backgrounds and lack of formal education, are regarded as being ignorant of family planning methods. Additional data on the actual practice of family planning among the informed are of significance. The Irish and West Indians were least likely to use family planning, 43.8 percent of the Irish and 42.9 percent of the West Indians compared to 63.3 percent of the English and 70.2 percent of the Indian/ Pakistani were classified as users.

Bearing in mind these data and the complex interrelationship of both rates with sociocultural and economic facts, the hasty conclusions drawn about colored birth rates and the alarming forecasts of future trends are neither reliable reflections of the present situation nor useful indications of future trends. From sociological evidence on population studies of communities living under varying structural conditions, we should not expect birth rates among colored groups to be permanently higher than the average for the total population. How these rates change and how rapidly depends, in no small measure, on the overall social relationships that develop between white and colored groups in Britain.

Race Relations and Immigration Control

As the restrictions on Commonwealth immigration have tightened, demands for stricter controls have been made. Proposals made for further limitations on dependents, the attachment of residential and employment conditions on those entering the country and the repatriation of colored people, are among those now put forward. The development of controls has been on an ad hoc basis of political expediency and not within a context of an overall immigration policy. This response to colored immigration and the continuing pressure for additional control has contributed in no small way to color awareness and the development of a race problem.

It is not the first time that immigration into Britain has created alarm and hostility. Such attitudes have been common enough and an analysis of earlier immigrations brings out many parallels with the present situation. The Protestant refugees from Europe in the sixteenth and eighteenth centuries were welcomed by the government but bitterly opposed by those who dealt with them. Tribute has long been paid to the skills they brought and the economic contribution they made, but this recognition was not widespread as they arrived speaking no English and often destitute. The Jewish immigration of the late nineteenth and early twentieth centuries and the Irish immigration from the end of the eighteenth century resulted in hostility and discrimination. In the twentieth century, settlement of Eastern Europeans, particularly Poles after World War II, was equally met by unfavorable attitudes, but the reaction was never wholly hostile. Each group gained some degree of acceptance; however, where differences persisted, although, for the most part latent, these possible sources of friction could be, and still are, used in certain situations as the basis of differential treatment.

The most obvious reaction to recent colored immigration was the introduction of legislative control of the numbers and kinds of immigrants. The clamor for such control was based on assumptions that immigrants could only be absorbed if they were relatively few in number, selected in terms of the needs of the host society, and geographically dispersed. The most extreme view was that immigrant entry not be allowed at all; however, so far, this position has received no official legal sanction. Migrations as a result of religious or political persecution are not likely to be orderly or steady, and immigrants who migrate for economic reasons, although more sensitive to the conditions in the receiving country, are not more likely than those fleeing from persecution to commend themselves to their hosts. The need for control was attributed to the migrants' characteristics, which were thought to be the cause of a variety of social problems. Although closely interrelated, the control and the social problem aspects need to be examined separately in order to understand the resulting consequences.

The campaign for the control of immigration prior to 1905 was similar in many respects to campaigns leading to the 1962 Act and subsequent acts. There were parallels in the exaggeration of the numbers and even though the immigrants were characterized by unfavorable stereotypes, such as being culturally alien and not assimilable, it was constantly denied that control was aimed at any racial or ethnic group. During the years 1875 and 1914, 120,000 Jews came to Britain, mainly as a result of economic, political, and religious persecution in Eastern Europe. Many more passed through Britain on their way to America. At the end of the nineteenth century only 0.69 percent of the population were aliens. (See Appendix IV for figures of aliens in England.) England has been described, at that time, as being in the forefront of lands of emigration but as a backwater of immigration—for each immigrant, England sent forth many emigrants.[51] Nevertheless, a Royal Commission on the Aliens Question was appointed with terms of reference relating to the control of alien immigration. In 1903 it reported and recommended control of alien immigration. Legislation was passed in 1905. Control applied not to Jews but to "undesirable aliens" who came to Britain on "immigrant ships" that carried more than twenty third-class passengers. In the campaign for control, allegations of crime, disease, and moral decay were made against the immigrants, and Jewish immigration was likened to the entry of diseased store cattle from Canada.[52] Two signatories of the "Minority Report of the Royal Commission" pointed out that because the Royal Commission had shown that there was hardly any diseased or criminal people among the immigrants, a bureaucracy was not necessary to keep out the diseased and the criminal. They also doubted whether bad character could be established by a few hurried inquiries or whether restrictive measures aimed at "undesirables" could be applied without affecting the deserving whose poverty on arrival was no reason to suppose that they could not attain independence.[53] Neither the evidence to the Royal Commission, which failed to confirm the unfavorable stereotypes of the immigrants, nor the "Minority Report," nor the organized opposition to control succeeded in preventing legislation. Whatever benefits accrued from such legislation, it has been argued that since legislation categorized groups differentially, by legitimating different treatment, the control of aliens also legitimated anti-Semitism.

The arguments in favor of control of entry of colored Commonwealth citizens frequently rest on a supposed relationship between numbers and problems. Both the problem of racialism and practical problems of housing, education, and the like are associated with the entry of colored people, although few are able to explain this relationship or have investigated under what conditions such a proposition is valid. Many remain satisfied either to reiterate the assumption as though it were proved or to accept it because it is heard so frequently. Some put the relationship in actual quantitative terms. Supporting the 1968 Bill, Lord Brooke said:

> If in Britain there was . . . to be created a climate in which community relations could be fostered, a limit to the rate of immigrants which could be absorbed must be accepted. The present rate of 60,000 a year is near the safe limit . . . if we are to avoid, as we have hitherto, a backlash from the native population. . . . Without the 1962 Act, race relations in some parts of this country would before now, have reached explosion point . . . . Those who opposed the 1968 Bill would be answerable at the bar of history for the explosions that would follow in towns and cities where the numbers of immigrants have reached near-saturation point.[54]

This is a dubious argument on two counts. We can neither assume that more colored people means more likelihood of trouble nor that fewer means less likelihood of violence. We have no evidence that 60,000 a year is safe, nor do we know what the saturation point is in any town or city. Are 10 colored people in one street or 50 children in one school or 5,000 in one city too many? Would 5, 25, *or* 2,500 prevent trouble? The relations between people of different ethnic origins and the conditions underlying violence or its absence cannot be related simply to numbers.

It has been argued that "inter-ethnic tension and conflict are found in changing societies. In situations in which the colour-line has not yet been established or where it is breaking down, there is disagreement over the relative position of ethnic groups."[55] Whether or not such conflict leads to violence depends not on numbers but on such immediate factors as the behavior of the police and local officials and longer term developments in the accepted modes of conduct toward minority groups. If, through redefinition, members of a minority group have been put in a vulnerable position, accused of causing or exacerbating problems, then the normal sanctions against violence may be waived when they are the victims. One contribution to such a situation is by selective presentation of activities of members of ethnic groups and the encouragement of derogatory stereotypes.

Colored immigration to Britain, involving relatively small numbers of migrants, has produced a reaction of disproportionate significance. The explanation of this reaction must be sought primarily in the structure of British society. The highly stratified population, continuing economic difficulties, and long-standing social problems, rather than the particular characteristics of the migrants, generate points of conflict that are then focused on minority groups.

Notes

[1] Letter to the London *Times*, May 6, 1967.

[2] See, for instance, H. P. Fairchild, *Immigration: A World Movement and Its American Significance*, rev. ed. (New York: Macmillan, 1925).

[3] William Petersen, "A General Typology of Migration," *American Sociological Review*, 23, no. 3 (June 1958), 258.

[4] *Ibid.*, pp. 256–266.

5 For the point on the advertising by employers, see G. M. Garland, "The Economic and Geographical Significance of the Commonwealth Immigrant Population in Bradford" (unpublished thesis, University of York, 1967), p. 12. For reference to the construction of the Mangla Dam in Mirpur District that displaced large numbers of peasant farmers, see John Goodall, "The Pakistani Background," in Robin Oakley (ed.), *New Backgrounds*, published for the Institute of Race Relations (London: Oxford University Press, © Institute of Race Relations, 1968), p. 73.

6 Petersen, *op. cit.*, p. 263.

7 For a discussion of these communities, see Sydney F. Collins, "The Social Position of White and 'Half-Caste' Women in Coloured Groupings in Britain," *American Sociological Review*, 16, no. 6 (December 1951), 796–802; "Social Processes Integrating Coloured People in Britain," *British Journal of Sociology*, 3, no. 1 (March 1952), 20–29; Kenneth Little, *Negroes in Britain* (London: Routledge and Kegan Paul, 1948); A. H. Richmond, *Colour Prejudice in Britain* (London: Routledge and Kegan Paul, 1954).

8 Hamza A. Alavi, *Pakistanis in Britain* (London: London Council of Social Service, 1963), p. 1.

9 Rashmi Desai, *Indian Immigrants in Britain*, published for the Institute of Race Relations (London: Oxford University Press, © Institute of Race Relations, 1963), p. 4. Reproduced by permission.

10 F. Marie Richards, "Third Generation Immigrants." Paper read to the Annual Conference of the National Association for Maternal and Child Welfare, mimeographed Cardiff, June 1967.

11 C. Konpadi, *Indians Overseas 1838–1949* (New Delhi: New Delhi Indian Council of World Affairs, 1949), p. 360.

12 Kingsley Davis, *The Population of India and Pakistan* (Princeton, New Jersey: Princeton University Press, 1951), p. 99.

13 Within the general economic context of overpopulation, lack of employment opportunities, and low standards of living, there is a wide variety of particular factors within and between the different areas that also have their effect. For further details, see R. B. Davison, *West Indian Migrants* (London: Oxford University Press, 1962); "Man-Land Relations in the Caribbean Area," in Vera Rubin (ed.), *Caribbean Studies: A Symposium* (United Commonwealth of the West Indies: Institute of Social and Economic Research, 1957), pp. 14–21; Mary Proudfoot, *Britain and the United States in the Caribbean* (London: Faber and Faber, 1954); G. E. Cumpner, "Labour Demand and Supply in the Jamaican

Sugar Industry," *Social and Economic Studies*, 2, no. 4 (March 1954), 37–86; "Working Class Emigration from Barbados to the U.K. October 1955," *Social and Economic Studies*, 6, no. 3 (September 1957), 165–77; "Employment in Barbados," *Social and Economic Studies*, 8, no. 2 (June 1959), 105–146; Konpadi, *op. cit.*, 1949; M. N. Srinivas, *Caste in Modern India and Other Essays* (New York: Asia Publishing House, 1962), pp. 77–86, pp. 120–135; S. C. Dube, *India's Changing Villages* (London: Routledge and Kegan Paul, 1958); M. Habibullah and A. Farouk, *The Pattern of Agricultural Unemployment* (Dacca: Bureau of Economic Research, Dacca University, 1962); *Village Life in Lahore District* (Lahore: Social Sciences Research Centre, University of Panjab); *Village in an Urban Orbit* (Lahore: Social Sciences Research Centre, University of Panjab, 1960); *The Budhopur Report* (Lahore: Social Sciences Research Centre, University of Panjab, 1962).

[14] Davison, *op. cit.*, p. xiii.

[15] Petersen, *op. cit.*, p. 259.

[16] *Ibid.*, p. 259.

[17] Ceri Peach, "West Indian Migration to Britain: The Economic Factors," *Race*, 7, no. 1 (July 1965), 45. Though less evidence is available for Indian and Pakistani dependents, my own research leads to similar conclusions. The wives, children, and parents represent a cost not only in fares but in upkeep in the United Kingdom and this calls for regular and adequate employment.

[18] Norman Pannell and Fenner Brockway, *Immigration, What is the Answer?* (London: Routledge and Kegan Paul, 1965), p. 8.

[19] For a full account of this period, see Ruth Glass, *Newcomers, The West Indians in London* (London: G. Allen and Unwin, 1960), pp. 133–146.

[20] Reproduced from the London *Times*, September 16, 1958 by permission.

[21] Paul Foot, *Immigration and Race in British Politics* (Baltimore: Penguin, 1965), p. 169.

[22] Reproduced from the *Daily Sketch*, London, September 2, 1958 by permission.

[23] See House of Commons Parliamentary Debates. *Weekly Hansard*, no. 476, Cols. 796–801 (London: H.M.S.O., January 29–February 4, 1960).

[24] *Parliamentary Debates*, House of Commons, Col. 1563 (London: H.M.S.O., December 5, 1958). Reproduced by permission.

[25] *Birmingham Evening Despatch*, December 8, 1959 in Foot, *op. cit.*, p. 197. Reproduced by permission.

[26] Sixty-two members of Parliament voted against the second reading of the bill: thirty-five Labour, fifteen Conservative, twelve Liberal, one Scottish, and one Welsh Nationalist member (Times, February 29, 1968). The government majority was 310 and the majority in the House of Lords was only 24 (*The Guardian*, March 2, 1968).

[27] Lord Elton, *The Unarmed Invasion* (London: Geoffrey Bles, 1965), p. 7.

[28] "Written Answers," *Hansard*, Col. 338 (London: H.M.S.O., June 22, 1967).

[29] Kenneth Leech, "Migration and the British Population, 1955–1962," *Race*, 7, no. 4 (London: Oxford University Press, April 1966), 402.

[30] Councillor Finney in Nicholas Deakin (ed.), *Colour and the British Electorate 1964* (London: Pall Mall Press, 1965), p. 91.

[31] ". . . one of the primary reasons for this sudden spurt in migration . . . is the rising clamour in Britain that the migration should be restricted!" (Davison, *op. cit.*, p. 7). "The record 1961 totals may also be attributable in part, at least, to the impending threat of legislative controls, which stampeded many into migrating at once before the door should close." (Sheila Patterson, *Dark Strangers* [London: Tavistock Publications, 1963], note 1., p. 43).

[32] Peach, *op. cit.*, p. 45.

[33] For a short but useful explanation of some of the differences between aliens and Commonwealth citizens, see Cedric Thornberry, *Stranger at the Gate*, Fabian Research Series 243 (London: Fabian Society, August 1964). See also Cedric Thornberry, "Discretion and Appeal in British Immigrant Law," *Institute of Race Relations Newsletter* (November 1965), pp. 30–33.

[34] David Renton, December 5, 1958 in Paul Foot, *op. cit.*, p. 125.

[35] *Ibid.*, p. 154.

[36] *Institute of Race Relations Newsletter* (London: Institute of Race Relations, October 1966), p. 7.

[37] Letter to the London *Times*, October 28, 1967.

[38] "Economist Intelligence Unit," *Commonwealth Immigration*, February 1967, p. 1.

[39] *Ministry of Labour Gazette*, 75, no. 3 (London: H.M.S.O., March 1967), 223.

[40] *Report of the Committee on Immigration Appeals*, Cmnd. 3387 (London: H.M.S.O., August 1967), p. 9.

[41] *Ibid.*, p. 20. *"Instruction to Immigration Officers,"* Cmnd. 3064, 1966 superseded Cmnd. 1716 and is the current version.

[42] F. Kafka, *The Castle* (London: Penguin Books, 1957), p. 75. The analysis of the situation of an individual in relation to bureaucratic powers is brilliantly and incisively portrayed in the position and responses of the land surveyor in this work.

[43] *Report of the Committee on Immigration Appeals, op. cit.*, p. 9.

[44] For cases typical of those in which entry was challanged, see "Economist Intelligence Unit," *Commonwealth Immigration*, April 1967, and National Council for Civil Liberties, *Annual Report* (London: 1966).

[45] *Sunday Telegraph*, April 9, 1967.

[46] For a critical examination of the official evidence on evasions and its manner of presentation, see Peter Norman, "Who Is Guilty of Evasion?", *Institute of Race Relations Newsletter* (November 1965), pp. 10–13.

[47] Richard Hooper (ed.), *Colour in Britain* (London: British Broadcasting Corporation, 1965), p. 21.

[48] Davis, *op. cit.*, 1951; *The World Social Situation*, United Nations Reports (New York: United Nations, 1952 and 1957).

[49] For the sociological treatment of population, see Kingsley Davis, *Human Society* (New York: Macmillan, 1949), chapters 20–21; Dennis H. Wrong, *Population*, rev. ed. (New York: Random House, 1959).

[50] J. A. H. Waterhouse and Diana H. Brabban, "Inquiry into Fertility of Immigrants, Preliminary Report," *Eugenics Review*, 56, no. 1 (April 1964), 7–18.

[51] Lloyd Gartner, *The Jewish Immigrant in England 1870–1914* (London: G. Allen and Unwin, 1960), p. 15.

[52] Paul Foot, *op. cit.*, p. 89.

[53] *Ibid.*, p. 92.

[54] Reproduced from the London *Times*, March 1, 1968 by permission.

[55] Tamotsu Shibutani and Kian M. Kwan, *Ethnic Stratification, A Comparative Approach* (New York: © *Copyright*, THE MACMILLAN COMPANY, 1965). p. 401. Reproduced by permission.

Chapter 3 ◉ The Social Organization of Immigrant Groups

In examining some of the main characteristics of the internal social organization of the three major groups of colored immigrants living in Britain at the present time, it should not be assumed that these groups can be conceptualized as being closed systems of social relations. The internal organization of each group has to be seen in relation to the new environment. There is neither total separation nor total identification with the dominant structure. In one sense, the groups are already part of the new environment, interpenetrating with it in various ways. In another sense, they can be considered as having some identity of their own, separated by different beliefs and customs and different interests and values. Adult migrants experience processes of resocialization that may result in changed ways of behaving or may serve to strengthen their adherence to traditional beliefs and practices. Some changes at the levels of personality and social relationships are involved in migration. The influence of a new environment varies in its impact on the structure of the family, kinship, and political and economic relationships, for instance. Changed conditions of living provide opportunities for new forms of social relationships. Whether these are adopted through necessity or through conscious intention, they have consequences for the social organization of the group.

It is possible that those who are highly motivated to migrate are those who have partially rejected traditional ways of behaving or whose allegiance to customary practices and beliefs is weakly developed. Their receptivity to the influences of the new environment may therefore be greater than those who migrate involuntarily. It cannot be assumed that their values and ideas are simply reflections of changed conditions, they may be prior to them.* New beliefs and actions are developed and communicated through social interaction, just as "old" ways are perpetuated through it. Within the immigrant groups in Britain aspects of both persistence and change are evident.

Many changes are involved in moving from a predominantly rural agricultural economy to an industrial urban setting. In the former, traditional patterns of behavior are legitimated and structured by the total environment; in the latter, few such structural supports for these patterns are found. For example, in rural India respect for age is rooted in a structure where age confers religious superiority, political influence, and control over the distribution and organization of joint economic resources.

> Younger members of the family have the utmost respect for their elders. Age is a mark of wisdom; youth a mark of inexperience. All orphans, widows and aged members of the family are cared for by others. The head of the family has authority over other members of it, even those who are married and are themselves fathers.[2]

This attitude of respect may be retained when people from this background migrate, but many of its structural supports disappear. For instance, younger adult members of the family may be economically more successful than older members, and they are frequently not dependent on kin ties for their occupation. The children of a family may be the only ones who acquire a high degree of fluency in English and take on the role of inter-

---

* Many explanations of social change have stressed the important perspective that changes in structural conditions bring about changes in ideas and these explanations have tended to reject ideational explanations of social change. Weber's position on the problems of social change and the role of ideas remains one of the most interesting and fruitful approaches. In the *Protestant Ethic* he says, "But it is of course, not my aim to substitute for a one-sided materialistic an equally one-sided spiritualistic causal interpretation of culture and of history. Each is equally possible, but each, if it does not serve as the preparation, but as the conclusion of an investigation, accomplishes equally little in the interest of historical truth."[1]

preters for their elders. In such a situation the retention of previous ways of thinking and behaving, however highly valued by the group, encounters obstacles.

In general terms, such conflicts between traditional and innovatory situations exist on many different levels and are expressed in many different ways. It is necessary to look at particular processes of social change to establish under what conditions traditional ways of behaving survive, what functions they serve in the new situation, and how far conscious attempts by groups to preserve certain patterns are effective. The processes by which changes occur are not usually consciously perceived or expressed. Some patterns of behavior may be more easily transferred from one situation to another, but these are not necessarily those most highly valued by the group. The changes themselves, where a highly valued form of behavior is questioned or begins to fall into disuse, are seen as shortcomings of the individuals in the situation and are a source of conflict within the family or the group.[3]

SETTLEMENT PATTERNS

The exact geographical distribution of West Indian, Indian, and Pakistani immigrants throughout Britain is not known. There are many difficulties in collecting such data. While census returns are required by law and penalties can be imposed for failing to give accurate information, many colored immigrants live in overcrowded conditions and do not wish this fact made known to local government officials. Commenting on the 1961 figures, R. B. Davison says:

> The secrecy of the census forms and the distinction between one set of government officials and another are not clearly understood by many recent arrivals, particularly coloured people who do not speak English. The accuracy of the census returns, in such cases, depended to no small extent upon the zeal of the enumerator who had to collect the schedule, and this was probably not uniform throughout the country. There is, therefore, a strong possibility that the under-counting of some immigrant groups

was much more serious than amongst the population at
large.[4]

In addition, it cannot be assumed that the immigrant population is geographically immobile after arrival in Britain. Indeed,
it is thought by many textile employers in the West Riding of
Yorkshire that mobility to the more affluent areas of the Midlands is characteristic of those who initially work in the textile
mills. This may be true; however, tracing mobility is highly
speculative and often tends to be based on a negative index of
the numbers who remain in areas over a considerable time.
This is not a very useful means of assessment. With continuing
immigration from overseas, those who move from one area to
another may well be replaced by new arrivals.

Despite the inadequacy of much of the data, several general
features of the situation can be distinguished. The colored immigrant population is not uniformly spread throughout Britain.
It would be surprising if it were. The whole population, white
and colored, is heavily concentrated in a few urban areas.
Within these areas, the ten largest cities account for just under
half of Britain's colored immigrants, according to one estimate.
Nearly twenty other cities and towns, varying in size from
54,060 (High Wycombe) to 267,050 (Leicester), had estimated
colored populations of 3,000 at the end of 1964.[5] At that time,
about 55 percent of the Indians in the country, 68 percent of
the Pakistanis, and almost 80 percent of the West Indians were
in six main urban regions.[6] (See Map 4 in Appendix.) About
half the West Indian population was resident in the greater
London area alone. In total, then, more than three-quarters
of the colored population made their homes in these urban
areas, whether conurbations, towns, or cities. The continued
immigration since 1964, while adding in some areas to the total
population of colored people, is unlikely to have altered the geographical distribution to any significant extent, particularly
since many new arrivals are dependents of people already there.

The settlement pattern according to ethnic origin shows some
variations. Most areas have people from all three groups, but
the ratios vary considerably. (See Map 4 in Appendix.) In one
area, Pakistanis will far outnumber the Indians and West In-

dians; in another, the West Indians or Indians will predominate. Such distributions have interesting effects on myths and stereotypes held by the native white population and are also closely related as cause and consequence to the internal social organization of the different ethnic minorities.

SETTLEMENT WITHIN URBAN AREAS

An understanding of settlement patterns within urban areas helps us to comprehend the kinds of social relationships existing within each minority group. Does the settlement pattern facilitate or hinder the maintenance of traditional forms of relationship? Does it encourage the growth of new forms of social relationships between members of the same ethnic minority? Before considering these questions, it is necessary to look briefly at some of the pressures that produce the existing patterns of settlement. It should not be assumed that these are the result only of traditional ethnic ties.

Urban residential patterns are not random. They are the outcome of the availability of accommodation and the attributes, supposed or real, of those seeking it. In general terms, Britain has an acute housing shortage in terms of quantity and the substandard quality of much that already exists. One in twenty families in England and Wales is sharing with other families and five and a half million houses are in need of replacement.[7] The competition for available houses is weighted heavily in favor of certain groups. Higher income groups are better placed to obtain accommodation and to get proportionately greater value for their money than those in lower income groups. It is said that "The typical British worker can get champagne if he wants it, but he cannot get decent housing."[8] In the sphere of public provision "social need," defined in a variety of ways by different local authorities, is supposed to be considered along with an ability to pay. Yet very rarely is social need, regardless of economic standing, the dominant consideration. The market for housing, both public and private, is highly competitive, especially in large cities and areas of economic development. Middle and lower income groups increasingly compete for the available accommodation and those in these groups with children, particularly large families and new arrivals, whether white or colored, are at a disadvantage. Therefore, people are not distributed regardless of their economic class position, social status, or the color of their skin.

Despite the concentrations of immigrants in certain areas, strictly defined ghettos have not been produced, but there is a growing indication that they may well appear in the future. Professional people, such as doctors and teachers from Asia and the West Indies, may be found living in "desirable residential areas," usually in the suburbs. Still colored people in the middle income range are usually subject to obstacles that a white person with the same position would not meet. The intensity with which these obstacles are applied varies greatly with the actual situation. Cases like that of a West Indian who was refused permission to buy a £3,500 house by the builder, although he had arranged a 90 percent mortgage and put down a deposit, are, by no means, uncommon.[9] Opposition can come from people already in the area, those concerned with selling the property, the builder or estate agent, the house owner himself, or those who supply financial backing in the form of mortgages. For those who require rented accommodation and those in lower income groups, particularly manual workers, the obstacles are formidable.[10]

At the time of the 1961 Census the colored population in towns was dispersed so that there was no one area of colored concentration as there had been of Jewish concentration in some districts of the East End of London or parts of Manchester or Leeds at the end of the last century.* Nevertheless, cluster-

---

* The term "ghetto" is frequently used in an undefined pejorative sense in the British press.[11] Even if the component of enforced residence that the term originally carried is ignored, two possible meanings can be given to it. First, it can be used descriptively for a district where the majority of the population is composed of an ethnic minority. In 1961 there was no borough in Britain that had more than 11 percent colored immigrants and few enumeration districts where colored immigrants were over 15 percent of the population. Any ghetto in this sense then is, at most, a few streets. Second, the term can be used to describe a situation in which the majority of any ethnic minority is concentrated in one district, regardless of the total composition of that district, where they may still form a minority. The term could be

ing was occurring and the evidence collected in a variety of towns, since 1961, indicates that such clusters have become more pronounced.[12] In Bradford, for example, the concentration of immigrants follows the pattern of Irish settlement in the mid-nineteenth century. Allowing for demolition, maps of Irish and colored distribution show a remarkable similarity. In some cases the houses are the same ones.[13]

There is an element of enforced residence in this clustering which can be attributed to the shortage of accommodation, the economic position of many immigrants, and the practices of those in control of the housing market. All these elements apply also to sections of the white population, but the last one may be practiced in reverse. It is becoming increasingly difficult for white house buyers to obtain mortgages for houses that are in areas designated as "colored" by those responsible for lending money. Although only of marginal significance to the white population, such practices increase the concentration and segregation aspects of residence patterns. The concentrations of colored immigrants are still characteristic of streets or parts of streets rather than whole districts.[14]

The concentrations, while varying in detail from town to town, show certain similarities. The following description is typical of the many accounts now existing of immigrant housing:

> The core area of Commonwealth immigrant settlement extends in a north-south zone immediately adjacent to the western fringe of the town centre. . . . This is predominantly an area of large early and mid-Victorian terrace houses with over five rooms, attics and basements, substantially built in stone, intermixed with smaller through-terrace houses of the same period. The former type has long undergone functional changes—on the main thor-

used in this second sense for the Whitechapel and St. George areas of London, in 1881, when 77.5 percent of London's Polish and Russian immigrants lived there. The term could also be used for Stepney in 1901 when out of 53,537 Russians and Poles in London, 42,032 were in Stepney. However, these were still not ghettos in the first sense of the word.

oughfares into offices, and in the back streets to lodging houses which accommodated earlier immigrant groups, especially the Irish and Poles. Lodging houses accommodating each Commonwealth immigrant group are intermixed in this area, but only rarely are different ethnic groups found in the same house, the main exception being Sikh landlords with West Indian tenants. Whilst many of the smaller terrace houses have undergone changes in the ethnic origins of their occupants, relatively few have changed in function. Single Indian and Pakistani families predominate in this type of house, along with a variable number of male kinsmen living with the family. . . .

With the recent rapid growth in the number of Indian and Pakistani family units, dispersal to smaller family houses in the inner working-class suburbs . . . has taken place. This pattern frequently evolves into a number of ethnic clusters of mid-nineteenth century back-to-back properties with three rooms, a basement or cellar-head scullery and lacking basic amenities. Whilst very few Indians or Pakistanis were municipal tenants in January 1964, at least 45 West Indian families [under 2 percent of the West Indian population] were housed on Corporation estates, with a slightly larger proportion in owner-occupied single family houses in working class suburbs. But the pattern of West Indian dispersal has been predominantly towards larger houses, built at the turn of the century . . . which are suitable for multiple family occupation and are purchased by partnerships amongst kinsmen. The spread of lodging houses accommodating each group has followed a similar pattern and further intensified the pattern of immigrant housing.[15]

This description refers to an area where housing is relatively easy to obtain. It shows the initial residence pattern altering in a relatively short time as the composition of the immigrant groups changes and as earlier populations move out. It brings out the varying patterns of immigrant housing, the lodging house, the houses in multiple family occupation, and the single family house also accommodating male relatives. The low proportion of council house tenants is not unusual.* A survey in 1967 found that less than 1 percent of colored immigrants live in council houses compared to 26 percent of the white population living in rented accommodation.[16]

The process of settlement is neither exclusively one of dispersal nor of clustering, both are present. Where, however, the housing shortage is acute and the local councils do not pursue a positive policy toward the housing of colored immigrants, clustering is the dominant trend. The majority of colored immigrants are found in the socioeconomic group from which council house tenants are largely drawn. The policies of councils are increasingly crucial in modifying or promoting the patterns of residential segregation. Eligibility is determined in three ways: rehousing following slum clearance or redevelopment, homelessness, and acceptance on a waiting list for housing as a home becomes available. The availability and allocation varies from area to area but the processes allow, indeed necessitate, discrimination between and within each of the three groups. In general these processes have so far militated against the housing of colored people in a number of ways, some involving color discrimination, others excluding them, along with all newcomers to an area, white and colored. Positive policies to promote the housing of colored families in equal proportion with whites necessitate an awareness of the working of present policies and an ability and willingness to change them. There is little evidence that councils are likely to adopt new policies toward housing colored families.

MIGRANT HOUSEHOLDS

The composition of migrant households is affected by at least three sets of factors: the social composition of the migrant population, the traditional kinship and household forms, and

---

* Council houses are built by local government authorities and rented to tenants who fulfill certain criteria. The building program and administration, in terms of selection of tenants and level of rents charged, varies among local authorities. Central government direction is achieved through conditions imposed on financial loans, but local politics largely determine the housing policies.

the pressures imposed by the new environment. Though similarities exist between the three groups of immigrants, the situation of Asians and West Indians differs sufficiently for them to be treated separately.

Asian Households

The initial immigration was of young male adults who came to work in Britain. Most were married before they came. The usual pattern was for them to be sent by their families to join a settled village kinsman who would act as their sponsor. They in turn would subsequently sponsor other male relatives. They were highly mobile, moving to areas where employment was available and periodically taking extended holidays with their families left behind in India and Pakistan. Substantial changes have taken place since immigration control was first seriously discussed. As movement became more difficult, dependents were brought over. In many cases the first to come were adolescent male relatives, followed later by wives and young children. Men, particularly among Pakistanis, still greatly outnumber women, but, increasingly, family units of husbands, wives, and children are being established in Britain through continued immigration and because earlier immigrants have reached marriageable age.

INDIAN HOUSEHOLDS. Rashmi Desai describes the changes in household forms, as the composition of Indian migration altered:

> Most Indian residents in a house are connected to each other by close ties of kinship, residence in the same village in India or close friendships with a family basis in India . . . however, with the increasing arrival of families the pattern of living is changing. Instead of fraternal males it is the nuclear family which shares a bedroom. . . . As a result, single male individuals move out when families come in.[17]*

---

* This has led, at certain times, to fewer residents occupying one house but overcrowding in others. The overcrowding is aggravated where houses become reception centers for new arrivals, whether from India or from other towns in Britain.

Those who have come from India as adults were socialized in very different family and local units from those in Western industrial societies. The traditional kinship organization of the family, a local group of linear relatives, and a wider group including affinal relatives, along with the village and caste organization, were the basic structuring factors of this socialization. However, the widespread assumption that all Indians are brought up within joint families ignores the complexity of traditional family patterns and the changes that have taken place in many parts of India during the past two decades. The traditional joint family, comprising all lineally related males of two or three generations and their wives and children, is now uncommon. Although many lineal relatives may share one house, they do not necessarily live as one family. They live as nuclear units clearly marked off from one another; each unit cooking separately and farming their share of the land. Similarly, there have been modifications in village and caste organization. Villages have their "traditionalists" and their "progressives" so that different emphases are afforded to the rules governing commensality, standards of conduct between relatives, members of different castes, or covillagers, marriage practices, and so on. In times of crisis, the joint family structure, with its hierarchy of respect and norms of decision making, is likely to come into operation as a mechanism of social control. At other times, less weight is given to tradition and therefore, innovative action is possible. The complexity and diversity of traditional modes of organization, along with changes in Indian village life, provides a background, not of a static unchanging system but one in which considerable change has already taken place. It is in light of this experience of change that the social organization in Britain must be seen.[18]

The acquisition of a house and the way in which the household is organized is closely related to the social organization of the areas of India from which the people come. The relations between partners in house ownership and between landlords and their Indian tenants are economic to some degree, but they are always more than this. The sanctions against exploitation of tenants or fraudulent practices against partners, the division of living space, and the network of obligations involved in joint occupation are based on kinship-village ties and involve the status of those concerned not only in the migrant community but in India as well. In an environment where the dominant legal, economic, and kinship relations are antipathetic to such arrangements, the viability of these patterns is under pressure. Resort to English courts of law and individualistic motivation and habits are still not the norm, but they are not unknown in the Indian migrant communities. Pressures such as those from local authorities attempting to deal with overcrowding, for instance, are disruptive of customary internal household arrangements.

In the migrant situation, the more conservative elements of the family, caste, and village tradition may be given more weight than at home, particularly in so far as migration is experienced as a critical phase. Obligations to relatively distant kin, not necessarily recognized in India, may become crucial in the early years of settlement. Moreover, in an environment largely alien to their religious observances or arranged marriages, greater importance may be attached to such observances and stricter preparation considered necessary to preserve marriage rules. In such situations, the social control exercised by family members both in Britain and India is likely to demand greater conformity with traditional values. A further pressure toward the observance of religious norms derives from the claims to higher status that strict observance has legitimated in the traditional caste evaluation system.[19] It is possible that such claims will accompany economic betterment, the acquisition of education, and so on. How great such pressure will be in Indian communities in Britain is not yet clear. It is one factor among many others that can influence the kind of social organization emerging at present.

The social relationships in Indian households are subject to conflicting sets of pressures—one that emphasizes the traditional aspects of family, caste, and community life and the other arising from the demands of an urban industrial environment. These conflicting demands are likely to be even more strongly experienced by the children now growing up in Britain.

PAKISTANI HOUSEHOLDS. The household forms among Pakistanis in Britain vary according to occupational groups, to some extent with the region in Britain where they have settled, length of residence, and, most particularly, with the presence or absence of wives and children. This last factor is not independent of the first one and both are interrelated with attitudes toward migration. University educated and professionally trained Pakistanis, who also hold positions in Britain roughly equivalent with their qualifications, are more likely to live in small family units outside the areas of colored concentration. These family units, living within the prescriptions of Islam, frequently have wives and daughters who enter the life of the community to a far greater extent than those who remain within a "colored area." They do not observe strict *purdah* nor are they withdrawn from education or prevented from taking employment. Such family units are numerically insignificant but are regarded by some observers, particularly whites concerned with race relations, to be of extreme social significance. They are accorded deference but are not regarded as leaders or representatives by the majority of Pakistani residents in Britain. Their way of life is in many respects alien and their identification with the dominant norms of integration further widens the gap. Manual workers of semi- or unskilled grades (whatever their formal qualifications), whose wives and children are with them, maintain close ties with other Pakistanis even when they are spatially dispersed. They are more likely to live in houses which they are buying than in council property, though in some areas Pakistani families do occupy council houses and flats. Frequently the "nuclear families" have relatives, particularly male kinsmen, living with them. The family type household whether of the literate professional group or of the manual working group is not, at the present time, typical. It represents a trend which will continue as more dependants arrive.

The dominant household form which has emerged is a group of single men (usually married men without their families) who are kinsmen or close friends from the same district in Pakistan sharing the same language and religion. The single sex multi-occupied house is geared to the working life of the occupants. Apart from the kitchen and washing facilities and occasionally a sitting room, the house is divided into sleeping accommodation. Shift work, overtime and weekend work leave little time for recreation, and the necessity of saving money either to return home or to acquire property and bring over families gives little incentive to turn these houses into anything more than temporary lodging places. On the other hand, hospitality, the providing of accommodation and the supporting of kinsmen, is obligatory; so in the case of new arrivals, over-crowding of existing multi-occupied houses occurs. This may be temporary, but when the kinsman has difficulty in finding other accommodation or work to support himself, overcrowding becomes a more or less permanent feature.*

The complex of relationships existing within these house-holds can only be mentioned briefly. Kinship is a basic feature. The range of recognition of kin among Pakistanis varies with the district from which they come. But in all cases the range of kinship recognition is much wider than those regarded as kin by natives of Britain. Moreover, kin and village ties often merge, so that it is not possible for an outsider to distinguish blood cousins from village cousins.† Within the family father-

---

* Though difficult to define in practice a difference exists between over-crowding due to mandatory hospitality and that due to business enterprise. For the public health inspector, the consequences may be the same; for the Pakistani host and his kinsmen, they are very different. When councils have taken steps to prevent the spread of multi-occupied dwellings and to reduce the numbers in any one dwelling, the problem of housing becomes an acute one for single male immigrants. They cannot obtain council housing that is normally reserved for families and may be prevented, economically or through discrimination, from buying or renting accommodation. In some areas, particularly in the Midlands, this presents a continuing source of friction; in other areas, such as the West Riding, the supply of small back-to-back houses at relatively low prices provides some relief, but where redevelopment schemes are planned, councils have either to rehouse or delay development of what they have come to regard as "problem areas."

† This is a source of constant friction when dealing with immigration officials who, because of the law, have to distinguish between "real" relatives and those who are only called relatives. Many cases have occurred in recent years of boys coming as dependents to join their uncles or in some cases fathers who have been refused entry to Britain because proof of relationship could not be given. Although attempts to evade immigration laws are one factor in the situation,

son relationships are most important, reflecting the descent and inheritance system. Patterns of deference between older and younger kin are very marked in the domestic situation with the older brother, in the absence of the father, having authority over his younger brothers, even when the younger brothers are adult wage earners. At home, although all brothers inherit equally, younger brothers are expected to defer their rights in favor of the elder brother in order to avoid fragmentation of the land. It is not unusual in the Bradford area for this pattern of deference to exist even when younger male kinsmen are occupationally better situated than the older ones and where their command of English is greater. "Family members are expected to be loyal to the family. They are expected to show obedience to their elders.[20] Such a situation may not be able to withstand prolonged discrepancies between actual individual earning power, power derived from language skills, and all that such skills imply when dealing with those outside the Pakistani community, on the one hand, and the traditional kinship authority patterns, on the other. It is indeed true that cases occur of young Pakistanis who do reject such authority patterns, but they are still rare exceptions and are not only roundly condemned by kinsmen but the cost to the individual in breaking the accepted custom is very high.[21] He loses the support of his fellow immigrants, and the difficulties of living in an alien society without that support are immense.

The majority of Pakistanis in Britain are from rural backgrounds and it is not possible to separate economic, political, and religious alignments from kinship relations. Households formed along kinship lines also involve their members in economic, political, and religious participation with one another. This complex of relationships encompasses the activities of the individual to a much greater degree than is characteristic of

---

undoubtedly the fine distinctions drawn by the British laws are not necessarily understood by the would-be immigrant, his family at home, or the receiving kinsmen here and, even if understood, are not meaningful in terms of Pakistani kin and village obligations. Some attempts to deal with the difficulties that arise have been made recently but no widening of the recognition of mutual obligation, which does not form part of the British kinship structure, is envisaged.

other ethnic groups in Britain. Although work, worship, and receration may be physically separated from the household, these activities are frequently pursued in company with members of that household. Social relationships in the households of male kinsmen are regulated mainly by the norms of the village-kin community.

The arrival of women and young children has brought a return to the strict segregation of domestic duties but a continuance of many other activities in the same way as in a totally male household. The strict segregation of activities between males and females within the Pakistani household means that the male members eat, work, and spend their leisure time largely in the company of other men. The Pakistani husband is mainly a breadwinner and plays little part in management of the household or the rearing of young children. As with Indian households the presence of wives and children leads to a strengthening of traditional ways of behaving. The Pakistani wife in Britain is likely to find herself isolated from other female company which would normally be available in her home village and so is increasingly dependent on her children.[22] Such dependence leads to stress being put on the inculcating of values which support family relationships. Patterns of deference toward parents, the socializing of girls in preparation for marriage within the strict religious limits, the observance of religious customs, and the use of the mother tongue may be insisted upon as symbols of identification with the old way of life. This orientation is even more marked as migration is still regarded as a temporary expedient and most Pakistanis hope to return home some time. The emphasis in the processes of socialization is therefore toward life in Pakistan rather than toward the British way of life. The basis of such socialization lies in preserving the network of family loyalties.

The influences and constraints of the wider society are already making some impact, but are regarded in the main with suspicion as threats to the proper conduct of social relationships. The strains imposed on the Pakistani family are likely to increase with the second generation. In coming to terms with settlement, modifications are already being made. How far these will develop will depend not on the organization of the family alone but on the extent to which other institutional supports are built up by the Pakistani communities.

West Indian Households

There is much more material relating to West Indian settlement patterns and housing conditions than exists for Indians and Pakistanis in Britain. Much of this relates to the situation in certain London boroughs, although evidence from other areas is increasingly available.[23]

The residence patterns within urban areas, discussed earlier, indicated the tendency for West Indians to be housed in "twilight areas" along with other colored immigrants. However, there are discernible differences within the group according to socioeconomic status, the length of stay, and the presence of families. Although many or most West Indians in the early stages of migration tend to live in these twilight areas, not all of them do so, and many move out as circumstances permit. The migration of West Indians began earlier than the other two groups and, in the main, kinship obligation and reciprocity were structurally much less important. Kinship played some part in helping people to migrate, but, in many instances, migration was undertaken on an individual basis, even in the case of women. The position of West Indian women is one of the most significant differences between West Indian and Asian migrants. The ratio of females to males coming to Britain increased more rapidly than the Indians and Pakistanis and the imbalance between the sexes is least in this group. In Britain the household forms that have emerged can be understood in terms of the relationships existing in the West Indies and the situation that the migrants meet in Britain.

The evidence collected by R. B. Davison on Jamaicans in London shows quite clearly that ". . . the great majority of Jamaicans in the survey are 'clustering' in largely Jamaican households."[24] But of the 77 percent who were living in Jamaican households at the end of their first year in England, only 18 percent were related to the landlord, and, by the end of the second year, the proportion of those related had increased slightly to 22 percent out of a lower overall total of 73 percent.

Other studies show West Indians living in multi-occupied houses with ethnically mixed populations, where the West Indian households occupy only one or two rooms.[25] Sheila Patterson commenting on multi-occupied houses says, "The organisation of these 'cellular' households is informal, impermanent, and tenuous like most other forms of migrant association."[26] The units in these households may be either married couples or single women, with or without children, or single men. The occupants may be kin but, more frequently, come from the same island in the West Indies. According to the needs of the units, the relationships usually involve some form of mutual aid in order to ease the transition and the problems of day-to-day life in an alien society. Domestic help for single men, babysitting services for single women, and economic and social support, particularly for new arrivals, are part of the organization of such households. Similar arrangements may exist among those who move into separate houses within the same street or area. Dispersal to more distant areas involves a loss of some of these amenities, a fact that must be weighed against the better living conditions and the higher status accompanying such moves.

The structure of the family in the West Indies varies with socioeconomic status. Due largely to the legacy of slavery, legal marriage was confined to upper-class families and even in more recent years has extended only to middle-class and upwardly mobile groups. Among the rest of the population, nonlegal unions, both transient and stable, and units based on maternal kin are the normal pattern.[27] Marriage, as an institution, was associated with high economic status and elaborate ceremony, rather than as a necessary step to establish a family. Katrin FitzHerbert discussing working-class family life says, "Today it is still more important as a statement of economic achievement and class affiliation, than as a context for a sexual relationship, a shared home, or raising children."[28] It may be a stable nuclear family group of parents and their children, a unit of a man and woman with their children of the current and previous unions, or it may consist of three generations, a woman with her children living together with her mother. Each of these forms is also likely to include, at some time or other, the children of other relatives, particularly sisters or daughters. The role of the adult members varies with the type of unit. In a married home, the father assumes authority over, and responsibility for, the family; while in stable unions, the wife is likely to share in both responsibility and authority. More transient relationships involve the woman maintaining and caring for her children, with or without help from a male partner. In such situations the units are dependent for their functioning either on assistance, both financial and otherwise, from maternal kin or on a series of liaisons in which the male partner contributes. Maternal kin tend to play a dominant part in the lives of most West Indians, not only in childhood but well into middle age.

In small scale rural areas, despite the loose structure of the family, nonlegal unions are subject to some forms of social control. These do not operate so effectively in urban-industrial societies. Some West Indian migrants, arriving without their families, entered into transient unions, which were outside the scope of minimum controls that could have been exercised at home. Nonetheless, many factors in the new environment led to placing greater emphasis on stable unions. Among these factors were the relative scarcity of women, greater opportunities for women in regular employment, the constraining attitude of "white" society (particularly where children were involved), and the move to England, which, for some, constituted a form of social mobility. Among the Jamaicans studied by Davison, prior to their departure from the West Indies and after settlement in London, it was found that the proportion legally married rose from 22 percent to 52 percent after two years in England.[29] These two contradictory trends of greater degrees of legal marriage but less control over nonlegal unions exist together and have to be seen in relation to a multiplicity of pressures and counterpressures exerted on West Indian men and women in the context of British society.*

---

* These contradictions are not always fully appreciated by native Britishers who have to deal with some of the problems that arise. This was particularly so in the early years of West Indian migration when little was known of the intricacies of their social relationships and when disapproval of "immorality" was a common standpoint. This led to some serious misunderstandings that involved unnecessary hardships and humiliations. It was not, however, without its amusing incidents. In a case personally known to me, a welfare worker visiting

Economic independence for lower-class West Indian women is difficult to achieve in the West Indies, but in Britain those in regular work are able to attain a measure of independence. Women living alone or with children lack the direct support of their extended kin but are usually part of a multiple household that acts as some form of substitute. Women can therefore frequently send home contributions toward the upkeep of children left behind with mothers and sisters and are able to maintain children born in England. Services such as babysitting and cleaning bring in extra income, and social security benefits enable them to get by in times of difficulty. Problems, however, arise not only from the frequently cramped and inconvenient living conditions but also from the difficulties that face working mothers with young children on relatively low incomes, even when they are part of a multiple household. There are a number of pressures that, if not in this generation, in the coming one, will tend to reduce the frequency of these units. Apart from the trend to legal marriage among younger West Indians, which, among other things, will leave fewer kin able to help, the expectations of the women are likely to go beyond the exhausting and difficult task of rearing children on their own, and a greater recognition of the deprivations suffered by children is probable when comparisons are no longer made with conditions in the West Indies but with other families in Britain. Of course, such a trend may also mean that illegitimate children will increasingly be put in foster homes or given up for adoption.

The following example illustrates the pressure to conform to an "acceptable" household pattern and shows the kind of behavior toward others that is considered worthy of approval. One council gives loans for house purchase only on condition that the house will be an owner-occupied family house.

This condition can impose great strains on immigrant house owners in that they are so often surrounded by badly

---

a woman in the hospital for the birth of her second baby urged her to leave the father of her children and make an independent life and offered help toward suitable arrangements for the children. On the third day, the girl, not without some exasperation, said, "We have been married for three years, are you suggesting I get divorced?"

housed friends and relatives . . . . Immigrants *show great strength of character* in resisting these pressures. In Sparkbrook it is said that many West Indian families deliberately buy the smallest house they can find in order to combat this problem. Home ownership appears to bring about a remarkable change in the people themselves. They become part of the community and have a stake in it.[30]

Children left behind in the West Indies by parents who emigrated may eventually be brought over to England. Where the parents have other children, are remarried, or a part of a new family group, the newly arrived children, in addition to getting accustomed to an entirely new society, have to cope with major adjustments within the family. Many of these problems are not appreciated by the parents or by the schools that the children attend. Household patterns, which were a part of the economic and social environment in the West Indies, do not fit so easily into the conditions in Britain. The multiple household and the maintenance of close ties of kinship or island origin give temporary and partial support to the continuance of such patterns, but these are under considerable pressure from both the dominant norms of white society and the relationship between economic achievement and nuclear family units in the West Indies. How soon extensive changes occur will depend on how far the housing and general economic conditions of West Indians improve.

Relationships within migrant households and the distribution within urban areas can be attributed, to some extent, to choice along traditional, familiar lines. But they are also due to the sheer necessity for most of Britain's West Indian, Indian, and Pakistani residents to find accommodation in a market that is highly competitive and discriminatory. The National Committee for Commonwealth Immigrants in its 1966 Report said, "There is open discrimination in housing particularly in the private sector. Even when there was no intention to discriminate, the normal processes of administration seemed to result in the exclusion from housing opportunities of all but a few immigrants. They were at the end of most housing queues."[31] Given this situation we cannot assume that common residence always, or even mainly, indicates strong community ties.

RELATIONS WITHIN COLORED
IMMIGRANT COMMUNITIES

It is frequently assumed that colored immigrants to Britain are all the same. Distinctions between Indians and Pakistanis are often not made and all West Indians are thought of as Jamaicans. The category "colored immigrant" is almost a meaningless one, in view of the great differences between the ethnic groups and also within them. Thus far the differences between the groups have been considered in this chapter. Little reference has been made to the differences within each group.

Socioeconomic differences exist in all the groups. This not only affects chances in the housing market and therefore residential patterns, but it also affects the types of associational relations developed in Britain. Through education, employment patterns, and living standards, the middle-class West Indians who come to Britain have much more in common with the British middle class than with working-class or peasant West Indians. Many of the barriers between the middle- and working-class West Indians are maintained in Britain. In the West Indies there has been a fairly close relationship between color and class—the lighter the skin, the less Negroid the features, then the higher the person's class position is likely to be. This does not fully hold any longer, either in the West Indies or among West Indians in Britain, but these characteristics have not lost all their significance among immigrants, despite the growing importance of achieved positions in Britain.

Indians and Pakistanis do not lose their strongly developed notions of stratification when they leave their home countries. One of the most frequently heard grievances of middle-class Asian immigrants is that many whites fail to distinguish between the different class or caste positions of those in the same ethnic group. Furthermore, they rapidly point out the differences between themselves and "simple illiterate peasants."

For the most part, migrants judge each other by the traditional hierarchy. For Indians and Pakistanis this is likely to remain the case, as long as they maintain close relations with their own kin groups, because these groups act jointly to give support and also maintain control over the activities of any one, individual member. Group, not individual, mobility is the accepted norm. However, although the majority of Asian immigrants maintain the relative positions they held at home, discrepancies are emerging. These are still relatively insignificant as far as the internal hierarchies are concerned, but they are an important source of possible future changes. Many university educated Indians and Pakistanis, for instance, find their qualifications not recognized in Britain and have to take unskilled laboring jobs. They are then occupationally reduced to the same position as many of their illiterate, non-English speaking countrymen. On the other hand, particularly with the help of extended kin groups, some peasants with no industrial or educational skills do become landlords and accumulate property that places them in an advantageous market position. The actual circumstances in which migrants are now living are beginning to influence judgments. At present, formal relations of deference and respect largely follow the old pattern, but on the informal level of gossip and assessment, present circumstances are playing their part. These will be of greater significance to the generation now growing up whose life chances and life styles will be largely determined by the economic position achieved by their parents in this country. This situation is most salient and anxiety provoking for those whose work in this country no longer demonstrates the relatively higher positions they held at home. It might be argued that those who are relatively more successful in this country will be more likely to remain, while those who are unsuccessful will be inclined to return home. The disappointment and frustration of the unsuccessful is already being voiced; nonetheless, the difficulties of returning home when debt has been incurred for fares, when the amounts earned permit little accumulation, and when the admission of "failure" brings its own problems are likely to deter many from this step.

The division of the ethnic groups into middle-class and manual workers is important in the general context of the differential position of colored immigrants in Britain. It is less significant within the groups themselves. This is so because of the numerical insignificance of the middle class and also because of the social distance and general lack of contact between the two classes. Many of those who retain their middle-class status in Britain live in a world different from those of peasant or working-class backgrounds and different from those who have been unable to retain their middle-class life styles. West Indians and Asians in professional occupations may have little or no contact with the lives of their fellow countrymen who are living and working in working-class areas. There are exceptions, particularly among those who see it as their function to "help" immigrants to cope with their problems, either in a professional or voluntary capacity. These develop a special relationship of a social worker-client kind; otherwise, their lives do not coincide. In Asian groups, the growing number of small businessmen providing services within the local communities and the growing number of commercial employees of Asian banks, travel agencies, and so on have much more direct contact with the bulk of the colored immigrant population than do the professional and semi-professional groups. This relationship within the Asian group encompasses more than economic differentiation; regional and national ties, as well as those of caste and kinship, are frequently involved, buttressing the positions of relative dependence and superiority. West Indians use some of the services provided by the Asian businessmen. For instance, food shops catering for West Indians are frequently run by Indians or Pakistanis, and many clubs, used mainly by West Indians, are Indian owned and managed. Between the Asians and West Indians the relationship is a much more straightforward, economic one.

Within each ethnic group other distinctions provide the basis of many forms of social organization. Some of the major distinctions that affect the lives of Indians, Pakistanis, and West Indians will now be examined.

Indians and Pakistanis

For both Indians and Pakistanis, linguistic-regional differences are a major cohesive force for those sharing a common language and region and a divisive force in the ethnic group as a whole. The Indians in Britain are separated culturally and organizationally according to their place of origin. The majority are from the Punjab and these are sub-divided further into Punjabi Sikhs and Punjabi Hindus. The rest are predominantly from Gujerat (called Gujeratis) and of these the majority are Hindus with a small minority of Muslims. Gujerati and Punjabi are not mutually intelligible languages. The Gujerati Hindus are divided into castes. There are the Anavil Brahmans, of whom there are relatively few in Britain; they are of a higher caste than the artisan and agricultural castes who form the majority in Britain. The castes are recognizable by distinctive surnames related on the whole to the traditional caste occupation. Although no castes formally exist among Muslims, the Gujerati Muslims form a separate caste-like group in relation to other Gujeratis.

The Pakistanis are all Muslims but, like the Indians, exhibit great differences depending on the area of origin. The majority are from West Pakistan with a substantial number coming from Azad Kashmir, sometimes called Mirpuris after the district of Mirpur. The rest are from East Pakistan, a thousand miles away from West Pakistan. Except for religion and political membership of the same state, there is little in common ethnically, culturally, or linguistically between the groups of Pakistanis.[32] In fact, the Pakistanis from the Punjabi speaking areas of West Pakistan can communicate easily with the Indian Punjabis but not with their fellow citizens, East Bengalis or Mirpuris. Those from Mirpur speak a Kashmiri dialect, which has some affinity to Punjabi, but East Bengali has no affinity. Language cuts across national boundaries even though people from the same country cannot communicate. The Muslim religion too is found in both states, but the Indian and Pakistani Muslims are separated into different religious groups. Of the Indians, Desai says, "It would be true to say that the sense of community does not extend beyond the linguistic regional group."[33] This can also be said of the Pakistanis who, after partition, "had no common language; they dressed differently, ate different foods; they had lived under different forms of government. It is hard to imagine a more heterogeneous nation."[34]

National identity is thus not well developed for either Indians or Pakistanis. A Bengali, a Pathan, a Gujerati or a Sikh think and feel this to be their identity and only rarely think in terms of being a Pakistani or an Indian. Those from the villages of Pakistan and India, who make up the vast majority of Pakistanis and Indians living in Britain, mix mainly, if not exclusively, with members of their own linguistic-regional group. Their households, their workmates, and those with whom they spend their leisure are mainly drawn, if not from their own village, from among those who speak a common language and share a common religion. With long working hours, including frequent if not permanent night work, they have little leisure. Most of this time is spent in informal groups exchanging gossip, visiting kinsmen, and discussing problems either at home or in shops and cafes run by their fellow countrymen. Cinemas showing films in their own languages and places of worship are centers that serve as meeting places.

Attempts have been made to establish organizations which override the linguistic-regional divisions. So far these have been very transient and no such established organizations exist.[35] Voluntary associations of various kinds have been developed. Many of these tend to be confined to the professional elites and to some extent include small businessmen. Literary societies, organizations to promote cultural activities such as traditional dancing and music, and associations catering to women are examples. Organizations depending on religious affiliation such as Mosque committees and Sikh temple associations have wider support and participation.

There are well over thirty Sikh temples in Britain. These are used not only as religious meeting places but as centers for social and political activities. The Sikh men, one of the few subgroups commonly recognized in Britain because of their turbans, beards, and long association with the British army, all share the same surname *Singh* (lion). The orthodox religion demands that they wear five distinctive marks as a sign of their membership in a universal brotherhood, the *Khalsa:* these are *Kara* (a steel bangle), *Kesh* (uncut hair—making a turban necessary), *Kangha* (a comb in the hair), *Kachch* (shorts), and *Kirpan* (a short ceremonial sword). Although many still conform, there is a growing number who cut both their hair and

beards. The Sikh religion has a strong egalitarian history, growing, as it did, as a reform movement within Hinduism; the
women also share a common surname *Kaur* (princess).[36] The
Gurudwaras (temples) which help to preserve the cultural aspects of Sikh life, religion, language, and music, not only for
the Sikh immigrants but for their children, were also the bases
that initially made possible the growth of a relatively strong,
independent Indian Workers' Association.

Founded originally in the 1930s, the Indian Workers' Association of Great Britain was reorganized and centralized in
September 1958. The previous year Nehru had visited Britain
and advised one central association for Indians who were working in the country. Until that time, no positive interest had been
taken by the Indian High Commission in the problem of immigrants. The Association consists of local associations of at
least twenty-five members anywhere in Great Britain, and membership is open to all Indians over eighteen years of age who are
in the area of a local association. A general council, consisting
of all executive committee members of local associations, is the
policy making body under which a central executive formally
works. The national Indian Workers' Association claims a high
membership in its sixteen local associations; meetings of up
to 1,000, in some areas, are not unknown. However, despite the
willingness to accept as members all Indians, membership is
largely, if not wholly, confined to Punjabis. The aims of the
association are broad. They include the promotion of multiracial cooperation and activities against discrimination, as well
as the improvement of conditions of life and work of the members.[37] Particular emphasis is placed on cooperation with the
British Trade Union and the Labour movement. The success of
these aims varies with local associations and differences have
arisen between local areas due to clashes of interpretation and
implementation, as well as dissensions connected with the
changing politics of India. Factionalism so rife in Indian politics
has lead to breakaways from the Indian Workers' Association.
At present there is one national body but two powerful, though
localized, rival bodies operating. The Indian Workers' Association in terms of formal organization is closest to the forms of

political organization found in Britain. But the cleavages are still based on the interests and affiliations of national or local loyalties in India.

Indian Associations tend to be composed entirely of Gujeratis and are found in a number of towns in Britain. They are concerned largely with cultural interests, although some development in connection with welfare problems of immigrants is now becoming more common. Attempts to extend membership beyond the Gujerati population have met with similar difficulties as those experienced by the Punjabis.

The Pakistanis maintain an Institute of International Affairs whose main activities are directed outward to the British society and involve only a minority of educated Pakistanis. In addition, the National Federation of Pakistani Associations seeks to coordinate activities but is hampered, among other reasons, by the internal divisions in Pakistani groups. Several Muslim associations have arisen where there are substantial settlements and they cater not only to religious interests but help with welfare problems of the communities. They are becoming particularly active on behalf of children, instructing them in the Islamic faith and teaching Urdu and Arabic. They cater to Muslims from East and West Pakistan. Although East Bengalis have formed associations in some areas, they have far fewer than West Pakistanis. In Bradford, for instance, where about 40 percent of the Pakistani population is East Bengali, they have only one organization, The Pakistani People's Association. The West Pakistanis, on the other hand, have a multiplicity of organizations mainly concerned with cultural activities, cinemas, and so on. In the face of constant problems over immigration, particularly those relating to dependents since the Commonwealth Immigration Act and the 1965 White Paper, the West Pakistanis recently formed the Pakistani Immigrants Welfare Association. So far the Pakistani population of Bradford, the largest in the United Kingdom, has not formed an association that embraces people from all three regional groups, East and West Pakistan and Azad Kashmir. Although some local groups such as Muslim associations, Mosque committees, and the All-Pakistan Women's Association are active and involve local memberships, organization on a national level in Britain is extremely weak.[38] Political dissension along the lines of that existing in Pakistan finds expression in Britain as a further obstacle to closer cooperation between Pakistani groups since the divisions tend to coincide with the linguistic-regional divisions already existing.

In both Indian and Pakistani associations, the officeholders tend to be drawn from those who hold higher status positions such as shopkeepers, those with secondary or university education, teachers, and clerks. This is partly due to their literacy and knowledge of English, which facilitates the organization of activities, but it is their status position in the migrant group to which they owe their acceptance as leaders. In many Gujerati associations, for instance, the officeholders are from the Anavil Brahman caste. In the Pakistani People's Association, mentioned above, all those in office have degrees. The Indian Workers' Association has drawn on a wider range of its membership to fill responsible positions. This widening of recruitment of officeholders reflects, to some extent, the outward-looking nature of the Indian Workers' Association. The status that an individual brings with him from his country of origin is a criterion fitting him for a leadership position so long as the organization is concerned with regional activities: teaching the children of migrants their mother tongue, organizing religious activities, preserving the artistic forms, singing and dancing, or arranging marriages. To the extent that the groups and subgroups of immigrant communities are still largely based on the distinctions deriving from the home situation, associations reinforce the separate communities. They preserve and maintain moral and cultural values and define the separate identity of the groups vis-à-vis each other and the white society. The associations may indicate "voluntary exclusion of the host society by immigrants" as Rashmi Desai claims, but the situation is not static.[39]

Increasingly, settlement in Britain is challenging the old way of life and the separate identities of the groups and subgroups. Leaders whose position is part of this old way of life can maintain their position only by preserving the separate identities. On the other hand, the problems of immigrants in employment, housing, and education call for leadership qualities and skills of a different kind. If associations attempt to deal with these problems, status in the traditional social organization may not fit individuals for leadership positions. Unless, for instance, a high caste Gujerati can also take on the functions and activities of a shop steward, he runs the risk of becoming irrelevant to a large area of problems that affect the lives of Gujeratis in Britain. If, on the other hand, associations do not attempt to deal with the everyday problems, they become increasingly divorced from the realities of life in Britain and, especially for younger Indians and Pakistanis, their activities assume a marginal significance.

The leaders of many of these associations are attempting to deal with the conflicting pressures by assuming representative functions in relation to the English authorities. As we shall later see, they are, at present, assisted in this by the acceptance of their leadership by local authority officials, government departments, and a multiplicity of committees that have arisen to deal with "immigrant problems." Many officials turn to these associations if they want the views or cooperation of immigrants. The ordinary members of immigrant communities are represented in the host society largely through the leaders of these associations. In turn, these leaders are expected to represent the views and demands of the wider society to the immigrant communities. In this sense it does not follow that "The more the immigrants participate in the associations, the more they abstain from activities in the host society."[40] For the leaders, at least, and through them for the members, increased contact with certain aspects of the wider society is involved in association membership. This wider contact, however, undermines the sectionalism on which many of the associations are based. Given this threat, greater emphasis may be placed, in some associations, on the cultural distinctions that identify and separate them from others.

However, the situation remains one in which everyday problems are a common experience, despite the many cultural differences. The skills necessary for dealing with these problems come not from the traditional background but from the knowledge and familiarity with the workings of British society. In this sense, immigrant associations are in a critical situation, calling for adaptability on the part of officeholders, the wider recruitment of leaders selected on the basis of different criteria, and, in most cases, a radical reorganization of the associations. These changes, however, are inimical to the aims of most of the existing associations.

The basis of new forms of organizations, with aims and activities relevant to the problems set by British society, lies in the common experiences in the new environment. Such organizations have so far experienced difficulty in overcoming the divisive factors of religion, language, and regional origin. Conditions already exist to bring about common action, but this is usually of relatively short duration and for specific purposes. During September 1967, a firm introduced alterations in working conditions that the employees perceived as detrimental to them. The employees, Gujeratis from India and mainly East Bengalis from Pakistan, came out on strike against the changes. For several days the strikers acted collectively and were represented by an East Bengali shop steward elected during the strike. They were members of a trade union but, in their view, were not adequately represented by it. Toward the end of the strike divisions appeared between the Gujeratis and Bengalis, the Gujeratis wanting to return to work and the Bengalis wanting to continue the strike. The Indians returned to work against the advice of the local Indian workers' association and the strike was broken. The welding together of traditionally opposed groups in response to common problems is still the exception among Britain's colored groups. There is, however, increasing evidence of such common action. The transformation of this action into more permanent organizations so far has not taken place.

West Indians

The West Indians in Britain cannot be treated in terms of their internal social organization as one group. There are class, color, and ethnic differences. In addition, the West Indians are migrants from widely scattered islands of the Caribbean and the former British territories on the mainland of South America. They continue to regard themselves as citizens of their territory,

Barbados, Trinidad, Guyana, and so on, rather than as West Indians. In households, at work, and in leisure-time activities, there is some evidence of distinctions made on an island basis. West Indian nationalism has a checkered history. There are physical, political, and economic differences that are important in the context of the West Indies. The rivalry between those from the larger islands, Jamaica and Trinidad, and the suspicion of those from the smaller islands toward them reflect these differences. Although place of origin plays some part in interpersonal relations between West Indians, it has not been, to any great extent, the basis of associational relations. This is partly due to the fact that while some groups, particularly the Jamaicans, are numerically relatively large and exhibit some geographical concentration, others are fewer and scattered. The Brixton area of London is predominantly Jamaican, whereas people from the smaller islands predominate in Notting Hill.

Social clubs of various kinds run by, and mainly for, West Indians have emerged, disappeared, and reemerged depending on local interest. Nonetheless, in most areas of West Indian settlement in Britain, the clubs have rarely involved more than a handful of local enthusiasts. Leisure-time activities are informal and pursued on an individual basis or with friends. Organizations concerned with the welfare of West Indian immigrants have frequently exhibited the same pattern. However, the Standing Conference of West Indian Organisations has done much to coordinate organizations and provides a source of information on West Indian opinion in some of the larger cities. The difficulties faced by these organizations reflect the situation in which West Indians find themselves in Britain. Although many of the problems they face are common to the majority of West Indians and other colored groups, they have other, seemingly more urgent demands on their time: they are internally divided by class, region of origin, and religious differences, and their priorities differ accordingly. Moreover, even if such difficulties can be overcome, there is no consensus on building up an internally cohesive West Indian community because, for many, the quest is some form of integration into British society. For instance, many West Indian associations concern themselves with a wide range of social and welfare activities for migrants and take active steps to combat discrimination, but their members are also frequently found in organizations concerned with integrating West Indians and whites in particular localities. This dual function still represents in large measure the dilemma presented to West Indians by British society. Increased evidence of discrimination at institutional levels, in schools, by local authority housing policies, in public and private employment, and at governmental level by legislation on immigration has brought some hardening of attitudes and, in some cases, has produced more militant forms of organization. One form this militancy takes is stressing the common interests and problems of West Indians and making it a basis for organization. The United West Indian Association in Sheffield in its journal, *For Love and Justice,* compared the efforts of Sikhs in Britain to organize politically with that of West Indians, and exhorted the West Indians to emulate them.[41] The stress on unity and action is brought out clearly in a speech at the opening of a local Afro-West Indian society:

> You see those kids there? Man, they're going to catch hell! . . . Because they are born in this country. They grow up in this country. They speak the same language. But they ain't going to get the same opportunities. And if anybody tells you "Yes," tell them that the days of fooling you to that extent have long been gone . . . we have experience now . . . children born . . . and educated here don't get the jobs they're entitled to . . . . I'm not an integrationist . . . . I cease to understand what they [integration and equal rights] mean . . . . Man, when the chips are down you're on your own. Every time. And the time has come now for black men and black women to unite and fight.[42]

Militant West Indian organizations, like the welfare orientated ones, so far involve only a few of the migrants. The leaders of the latter group of organizations are predominantly professional people, students, or long settled lower middle- or working-class West Indians. Their leadership, though unrepresentative, brought them into contact with the wider society and they were "acceptable" and "accepted" as spokesmen of West Indian migrants. The emergence of more militant leadership, while probably still unrepresentative, does not share in this acceptability. However, militant leadership reflects one important aspect of the experience of West Indian working-class migrants to Britain—their treatment on an unequal basis. This may prove to be a more strongly uniting factor than any other, giving the diverse West Indian groups a common identity.

Many West Indians have been deterred from activities that cost money. Saving to bring over dependents and accommodate them, as well as providing a reasonable standard of living for themselves consumes much of their time and energy. These demands have given rise to cooperative associations, often called credit unions, that enable individuals to join together for the purpose of saving and obtaining credit. In the West Indies these associations involve a wide range of reciprocal services between members of the group. In Britain they tend to be restricted to economic activities. Of such associations Sheila Patterson states, "These associations are groups of 'partners,' in which each member contributes a weekly sum and draws out a lump sum every so often. The accumulation enables him or her to make a down-payment on a house, car or other large purchase, or to send the fare home for a relative."[43] The associations also act as a form of insurance in times of economic hardship. Members who, for one reason or another, are in need of financial assistance can draw on the resources of the group and repay as their circumstances improve. These groups tend to be composed of members of roughly equal status, frequently known to one another in the West Indies. There are few West Indians in Britain with the kind of capital available that some Asian businessmen can put at the disposal of members of their Asian communities. The majority of West Indians depend on cooperative association with others in the same position.

Religion in the West Indies plays a vital part in the lives of the population, but the religious differences among the West Indians in Britain have not led to strong internal groupings on religious lines. Adherence to a particular religion derives largely from the historical development of different islands. Those territories settled first by the French or Spaniards, such as British Honduras, Trinidad, Dominica, St. Lucia, and St. Vincent, were Roman Catholic, while on islands such as Barbados or Jamaica, the early settlers were Anglican. These churches were associated with upper- and middle-class status. Status and color differences were more clear-cut in Anglican churches, but in Roman Catholic churches too, although more subtle, they appear to have had a place.* The intense missionary activity which began in the post-Emancipation period led to a multiplicity of Christian sects, Christian Science, Seventh Day Adventists, Society of Friends, Jehovah's Witnesses, as well as the splitting of the more conventional church into Baptists, Methodists, Congregationalists, and the like. This multiplicity and overlapping has been seen by some as an obstacle to the growth of the Christian movement in Jamaica. Nevertheless, Douglas Manley claims that "Jamaica is probably better churched and 'Christianized' than some parts of the world more commonly known as 'Christian.' "[45] In Trinidad and Guyana the introduction of indentured Indian labor has resulted in large Hindu and Muslim minorities. Even though the more established Christian sects met some of the needs of the poorer groups, the situation of extreme social and economic deprivation produced a variety of cults whose total membership was officially small, but a much larger proportion of the population participated from time to time.†

In the migrant situation, participation in some form of religious activity depends on several factors. The more secular atmosphere of Britain does not place the same stress on religious observance as does the background environment from which the migrants come. The competition of other activities and particularly the demands of earning a living leaves little time during the week; Sundays represent a chance to earn extra

---

* Michael de Freitas or Michael X, a Trinidadian, tells how his mother wanted him to be white like his Portuguese father: "She wanted me to serve at Mass, but at Mass only white boys served—black boys served at funerals."[44]

† Cults such as Revivalist Zion, Pocomania in Jamaica, and Shango in Trinidad combine African and Christian forms. They focus attention on the next world, using spirit possession and magic; the leaders claim healing powers. These processes give cult members and participants a sense of belonging to an elect group and make possible temporary withdrawal from the exigencies of the harsh world in which they live. Others emphasize withdrawal to a black African Utopia. While stressing monotheism, their beliefs and practices are political as well as religious.

income through higher rates of pay or a time to devote to the children and household. Sheila Patterson found that only a minority of West Indians participated in the religious life in Brixton; R. B. Davison reported that less than half the men and just over half the women in his survey claimed to attend church.[46] It seems that evidence from other areas confirms that, although most migrants arrive with a strong religious background, there is an overall slackening off of religious activity once in Britain.*

In addition to the general reasons given, there is a variety of particular ones. The atmosphere of English services, the behavior of the minister, or the white congregation may be felt unwelcoming or simply alien. The kind of church to which the migrant is accustomed may not exist locally or the migrant simply may not know how to contact such a church. R. B. Davison says a typical comment from the migrant was that he would "like to join a Pentecostal Church but doesn't know how to find one and is not interested in other types of church."[48] It is difficult to assess how far such comments are due to an actual lack of knowledge or are symptomatic of a change in behavior directed toward a less active interest in religion. Pentecostal sects have increased in many areas of West Indian settlement; for instance, in Bradford, an area with only about 3,000 West Indians, there are several sects meeting regularly. In some cases these have drawn people away from mixed congregations. The increase is partly due to the arrival of greater numbers of West Indian women, but it also reflects the socioeconomic background of most of the West Indians. Those who attend established churches tend to be drawn from middle- and socially aspiring working-class groups who have been settled for several years in Britain. The members of sects or cults are from lower socioeconomic backgrounds and the more devoted members continue their activities in Pentecostal churches here. The sects

---

* Calley found a disparity among Seventh Day Adventists, members of the Church of England, and Congregationalists. ". . . the tendency to transfer membership is much stronger among Adventists than in the other two denominations. The Adventist West Indian . . . does not seem to lose interest after being in England for a while, whereas both Congregationalists and Anglican clergy complain bitterly of this in their churches."[47]

that were already established before most of the West Indians came are not as successful as those established by West Indian migrant preachers. "West Indians have imported their preachers and their sects ready-made; they have not joined sects they found already operating in England."[49] Although these sects welcome English members their congregations in the majority of cases are totally West Indian. "Many more than half the members of the sects come from Jamaica."[50]

The position of cults in the migrant situation is not easy to ascertain. It is thought that few cult groups exist in Britain, but it is not unlikely that information of this kind of activity would be withheld, particularly from white investigators, for it is known that participation in cults is not approved. Discrimination may strengthen the appeal of such organizations. On the other hand, a decline in this form of religious behavior is likely to accompany migration when the migrants become relatively better off and social deprivation is not necessarily perceived as a permanent state by those of minority status.

CULTURAL DIFFERENCES AND THE NEW ENVIRONMENT

All migrations involve stress for the individuals and changes in the forms of social organization. The re-creation of familiar patterns of life through the preservation of customary social relationships is a feature of migrant groups, however small they may be. The security derived from such relationships is not only economic or social but also part of the individual's self-identification. The migrants to Britain over the past decade and a half who have come from colored Commonwealth countries have been no exception. Since, however, they come from diverse cultures, the relationships they have sought to preserve vary and, within the same ethnic group, a multiplicity of forms of behavior exist. Some of these they hope to pass on to their children through socialization within the family and within the associations, both formal and informal, so they are able to develop within the framework of British society. This diversity is, however, only part of the totality of relationships of colored immigrants. They share a common experience of living within a predominantly white society. Most of them work for white employers, their children attend schools with white children and teachers, and the mass media is oriented toward the values of urban, industrial white society. Lewis Nkosi summed the response to this experience when he wrote, "Black consciousness really begins with the shock of discovery that one is not only black but is also *non-white*."[51] Nonetheless, this experience and response is mediated for colored immigrants to Britain in terms of their own backgrounds. So the Sikh or the Muslim, in so far as he can re-create and retain familiar relationships, has an alternative value system, different, but not inferior to that of the white society. The West Indian, however, lacks this kind of alternative and is therefore less able to withstand the evaluation of himself as non-white. It is the paradox of the situation that those who are culturally least distinct from the indigenous British are made aware most quickly of the growing importance of color in British society.

Notes

[1] Max Weber, *The Protestant Ethic and The Spirit of Capitalism,* Talcott Parsons (tr.) (London: G. Allen and Unwin, 1930), p. 183.

[2] Hiro Dilip, *The Indian Family in Britain* (London: National Committee for Commonwealth Immigrants, 1967), p. 7. Reproduced by permission of the Community Relations Commission.

[3] For a classic study of migration and its effects, see W. I. Thomas and Florian Znaniecki, *The Polish Peasant in Europe and America,* sec. ed. (New York: Dover Publications, 1958). This work uses family and personal histories to illustrate and analyze the processes of social and personal disorganization and the effects of migration on family structure.

[4] R. B. Davison, "The Distribution of Immigrant Groups in London," *Race*, 5, no. 2 (October 1963), 56–69.

[5] Richard Hooper (ed.) *Colour in Britain* (London: British Broadcasting Corporation, 1965), pp. 15–19.

[6] Ruth Glass, "The Settlers: Where They Live," *Times*, July 1, 1965.

[7] For further discussions of the housing situation, see Stanley Alderson, *Housing* (Baltimore: Penguin, 1962).

[8] *Ibid.*, p. 10.

[9] *The Observer*, May 7, 1967.

[10] For further details, see *Report on Racial Discrimination* (London: Political and Economic Planning, 1967), section III, pp. 69–98; *Report on Racial Discrimination*, London Compaign Against Racial Discrimination, mimeographed, 1967, pp. 26–28.

[11] See "The Dark Million," *Times*, January 18, 1965; Nicholas Stacey, "How the Church Could Survive," *The Observer*, May 23, 1965.

[12] See "Area Reports on Cities and Boroughs with Substantial Immigrant Settlement," *Supplement to Institute of Race Relations Newsletter* (London: Institute of Race Relations, July 1965, September 1965, May 1966, June 1966, September 1966, and October 1966). These reports cover Sheffield, Glasgow, Bolton (Lancashire), Nottingham, Smethwick, and Huddersfield; Nicholas Deakin, "Residential Segregation in Britain; a Comparative Note," *Race*, Vol. 6, no. 1 (July 1964).

[13] C. Richardson, "Irish Settlement in Mid-Nineteenth Century Bradford," *Yorkshire Bulletin of Economic and Social Research*, Vol. 20, no. 1 (May 1968).

[14] See John Rex and Robert Moore, *Race, Community and Conflict, A Study of Sparkbrook*, published for the Institute of Race Relations (London: Oxford University Press, 1967), pp. 47–51; Rashmi Desai, *Indian Immigrants in Britain*, published for the Institute of Race Relations (London: Oxford University Press, © Institute of Race Relations, 1963), pp. 22–24.

[15] John Goodall, "Area Report on Cities and Boroughs with Substantial Immigrant Settlements No. 15 Huddersfield," *Supplement to Institute of Race Relations Newsletter* (London: Institute of Race Relations, © Institute of Race Relations, October 1966). Reproduced by permission.

[16] *Report on Racial Discrimination, op. cit.*, p. 69.

[17] Desai, *op. cit.*, pp. 30–31. Reproduced by permission.

[18] Some of these changes are recent, others are the results of much longer processes. Many of them are analyzed in M. S. Srinivas, *Caste in Modern India and Other Essays* (New York: Asian Publishing House, 1962), especially pp. 42–62 and pp. 87–97.

[19] *Ibid.*, pp. 56–57.

[20] Farrukh Hashmi, *The Pakistani Family in Britain* (London: National Committee for Commonwealth Immigrants), p. 7. Reproduced by permission of the Community Relations Commission.

21 Farrukh Hashmi discussing the contravention of accepted family patterns states, "On these occasions the family alters its supportive role from being a source of comfort and help, to that of a correcting force and a pressure group. Many Pakistanis who have invited displeasure of their families would prefer to spend the rest of their days in unhappy exile in this country rather than return home and accept the consequences." The consequences of course exist for those who are also here (*Ibid.*, pp. 9–10).

22 For a description of households in Pakistan and relationships emerging in the immigrant community, see Zaynab Dahya, "Pakistani Wives in Britain," *Race*, Vol. 6, no. 3, published for the Institute of Race Relations (London: Oxford University Press, © Institute of Race Relations, January 1965).

23 See R. B. Davison, *Black British* (London: Oxford University Press, 1966), Chapters II and III; Ruth Glass, *Newcomers, the West Indians in London*, pp. 32–43 and pp. 44–62; Ruth Glass and John Westergaard, *London's Housing Needs* (London: Centre for Urban Studies, 1965), particularly pp. 8–11 and pp. 34–44; Sheila Patterson, *Dark Strangers* (London: Tavistock, 1963), pp. 157–191 and pp. 259–300. These relate to London or, more particularly, to specified areas within London. Peter Collinson ("Immigrants and Residence," Sociology, 1, no. 3, [September 1967], 277–292) deals with Oxford. The study by Elizabeth Burney (*Housing on Trial: A Study of Immigrants and Local Government* [London: Oxford University Press, 1967]) gives valuable additional information on two London boroughs and Wolverhampton, Nottingham, Manchester, and Bedford.

24 Davison, *Black British*, *op. cit.*, p. 110.

25 See Rex and Moore, *op. cit.*, pp. 53–55.

26 Patterson, *op. cit.*, p. 347.

27 For a description of family patterns, see Yehudi A. Cohen, "Structure and Function: Family Organisation and Socialisation in a Jamaican Community," *American Anthropologist*, Vol. 58 (1956); Edith Clarke, *My Mother Who Fathered Me* (London: G. Allen and Unwin, 1957); F. M. Henriques, *Family and Colour in Jamaica*, sec. ed. (London: Eyre and Spottiswoode, 1963).

28 Katrin FitzHerbert, "The West Indian Background," in Robin Oakley (ed.), *New Backgrounds* (London: Oxford University Press, © Institute of Race Relations, 1968), p. 9. Reproduced by permission.

29 Davison, *Black British*, *op. cit.*, p. 30.

30 "Commonwealth Immigration," *Economist Intelligence Unit*, March 1967, p. 4. Reproduced by permission.

[31] Reproduced from the London *Times*, February 9, 1967 by permission.

[32] For a description of the differences in more detail, see R. D. Campbell, *Pakistan, Emerging Democracy* (Princeton, N.J.: Van Nostrand, 1963).

[33] Desai, *op. cit.*, p. 17. Reproduced by permission.

[34] Campbell, *op. cit.*, p. 7.

[35] For an example of one attempt to found such an association for all Indians in Britain, see Desai, *op. cit.*, p. 91.

[36] For further details of Sikh women immigrants, see Narindar Uberoi, "Sikh Women in Southall," *Race*, Vol. 6, no. 1 (July 1964).

[37] In the constitution passed on September 21, 1958 and modified on on February 28, 1959 the aims and objects of the Indian Workers' Association, Great Britain, are given as follows:
To organize Indians to:
i. safeguard and improve their conditions of life and work;
ii. seek co-operation of the Indian High Commission in U.K. towards the fufilment of its aims and objects;
iii. promote cooperation and unity with the Trade Union and Labour Movement in Great Britain;
iv. strengthen friendship with the British and all other peoples in Great Britain and co-operate with their organisations to this end;
v. fight against all forms of discrimination based on race, colour, creed or sex, for equal human rights and social and economic opportunities, and co-operate with other organisations for the same;
vi. promote the cause of friendship, peace and freedom of all countries and co-operate with other organisations, national and international, striving for the same;
vii. keep its members in particular, and people in Great Britain generally, informed of political, economic and social developments in India; and to
viii. undertake social, welfare and cultural activities towards the fulfilment of the above aims and objects.
Reproduced by permission of the Indian Workers' Association.

[38] Zaynab Dahya wrote, "There is no association or society in Britain to cater for the leisure-time needs of Pakistani wives . . . and there are vast problems—the *purdah* being only one of them—in organising anything comparable to the Indian Women's Associations which exist in various English cities and towns." Dahya, *op. cit.*, p. 320. Reproduced by permission. Some steps have been taken, usually by professional Pakistani women, to establish associations,

but, undoubtedly, these still affect very few women and the problems still remain.

[39] Desai, *op. cit.*, p. 107. Reproduced by permission.

[40] *Ibid.*, p. 106.

[41] *For Love and Justice,* Vol. 2, no. 4, mimeographed (April 1967).

[42] Report of a speech by Oscar Abrams, *Afro-West Indian Society Newsletter,* Vol. 2, no. 1, mimeographed (Bradford: July 1968), p. 1.

[43] Patterson, *op. cit.*, p. 301.

[44] David Knox, "Britain's Black Powerhouse: Michael X," *Life,* Atlantic ed., Vol. 43, no. 8, October 16, 1967.

[45] S. K. Ruck (ed.), *The West Indian Comes to England* (London: Routledge and Kegan Paul, 1960), p. 48.

[46] Patterson, *op. cit.*, pp. 303–304; Davison, *Black British, op. cit.*, p. 128.

[47] M. J. C. Calley, "Pentecostal Sects Among West Indian Migrants," *Race,* Vol. 3, no. 2, published for the Institute of Race Relations (London: Oxford University Press, © Institute of Race Relations, 1962), p. 57. Reproduced by permission. For a discussion on Baptists, see C. H. L. Gayle, "A Baptist Minister in Birmingham," *Institute of Race Relations Newsletter* (July/August 1966), pp. 21–27.

[48] Davison, *Black British, op. cit.*, p. 124.

[49] Calley, *op. cit.*, p. 58.

[50] *Ibid.*, p. 60.

[51] Gerald Moore and Ulli Beier (eds.), *Modern Poetry from Africa* (Baltimore: Penguin, 1963), p. 13.

Chapter 4 ⊚ The Development of Intergroup Relations

ETHNOCENTRISM AND DISCRIMINATION

Ethnocentrism has been defined as the ". . . view of things in which one's own group is the centre of everything, and all others are scaled and rated with reference to it."[1] The term is applied not only between societies where it is increasingly associated with nationalism but within societies to describe in-group attitudes, whether these refer to religious, economic, racial, caste, or class groups.

In Chapter 1 we saw how British society is a complex structure of interrelated groups with overlapping memberships but differentiated by familial, occupational, religious, political, and recreational ties. In Chapter 3 we examined similar divisions among West Indians, Indians, and Pakistanis. It was noted how these groups, both native and migrant, are related to systems of socioeconomic stratification that involve differential evaluations and life chances.

Prejudice and discrimination occupy a central position both in many analyses of, and in popular discourse on, inter-ethnic group relations. These terms need clarification if they are to be useful in the understanding of such relations. We know from psychological studies that differences do exist between individuals and groups in the amounts and kinds of prejudice they exhibit. A variety of scales have been developed to measure the intensity and distribution of these attitudes and a great deal of research has been carried out on how they develop, relate to behavior, and are transformed. Moreover, attention has been given to the typical traits of individuals who appear to be more intensely prejudiced than others, and attempts have been made to delineate personality types in accordance with these. The most famous is the study by Adorno and others, *The Authoritarian Personality*.[2] This study found that many highly prejudiced individuals are suffering from some mental disturbance. This finding is useful with reference to the extremely prejudiced, but it cannot explain the degree or type of prejudice found within the normal population. In many situations it is normal not only to express prejudice but to act in a discriminatory way against racial or ethnic minorities. In many other situations, such behavior is equally abnormal.

Prejudice considered as an irrational prejudgment, an attitude, may or may not be translated into action. Discrimination is overt behavior disfavoring persons or groups. It is often assumed that discrimination is based on hostile feelings and attitudes, that it is prejudice transformed into action. R. K. Merton formulated the various relations and combinations of prejudice and discrimination that illustrate this to be only one of a number of possible relationships. He expresses prejudice as nonconformity with the American creed and therefore uses a negative symbol; he sees nonprejudice as conformity with the American creed and uses a positive symbol (see Table 5).

Table 5.

	ATTITUDE DIMENSION: PREJUDICE AND NONPREJUDICE	BEHAVIOR DIMENSION: DISCRIMINATION AND NONDISCRIMINATION
Unprejudiced Nondiscriminator	+	+
Unprejudiced Discriminator	+	−
Prejudiced Nondiscriminator	−	+
Prejudiced Discriminator	−	−

SOURCE: Robert K. Merton, "Discrimination and The American Creed," in R. M. MacIver (ed.), *Discrimination and National Welfare* (New York: Harper & Row, 1949), pp. 100–101. Reproduced by permission.

This reformulation of the relations between prejudice and discrimination still leaves many questions unresolved. One recent study of inter-ethnic relations claims that the terms are:

. . . vague and laden with value judgments . . . . Although these words may be satisfactory for daily discourse, their use hinders systematic research . . . the making of distinctions of some kind is an essential part of all social life . . . . "Prejudice" designates an attitude of which the speaker disapproves. When a person avows a prejudice, he is saying that he holds views he cannot justify . . . . The two terms have diverse meanings because different people disapprove of different things . . . . Until these concepts are clearly identified generalisations cannot be formulated and tested.[3]

A recognition in general terms of the validity of these criticisms, the overemphasis on the terms, the vague and diverse meanings given to them, as well as the tendency to state and investigate inter-ethnic contacts as moral problems are crucial steps toward developing a systematic analysis of inter-ethnic contacts.

Two problems are frequently overlooked—intentionality and level of awareness. Discrimination on racial grounds that results from a conscious, rational attempt on the part of those in power positions, whether national or local elites, to subordinate minorities to their own interests is one important form of discrimination. Individuals in power positions may attempt and succeed in doing this, but the processes involved in the interrelations between dominant and minority groups are much more complex than this and usually much more subtle. Individuals who state that they do not discriminate or have no prejudice may be unaware of the consequences of their actions. This is not a question of dishonesty. The normal everyday routines of their occupations, for instance, may involve discrimination on racial grounds. Many policies, intentionally or not, have the consequence of such discrimination, even though the people involved have attitudes that are not prejudiced. It is one indication of the underdevelopment of the race relations situation in Britain that discriminatory policies are frequently not recognized as such either by those who devise and carry them out or by those who are the recipients. One possible explanation of this is the majority of Britain's colored population are fairly recent immigrants; the label "immigrant" can be used when colored is meant. When this no longer applies, with the second and subsequent generations, the realities of the situation will be clearer. How far and in what areas the term "colored" will be used cannot be accurately predicted.*

The attitudes and practices exhibited in normal populations involve a consideration of the socialization of groups to perceive themselves and others in certain ways, the sanctions to behave in conformity with established or emerging beliefs and values, and the relation of the content of such beliefs and values to the distribution of power within any particular situation.

Many studies of relationships between groups of different ethnic or racial origins start with an assumption that it is the ethnic or racial differences that explain these relationships. This implicitly assumes that the other factors in the situation are of less significance than the racial or ethnic ones, or it ignores the other factors altogether. In a sociological analysis, the operation of values that define some groups as inferior and some as superior cannot be analyzed simply in terms of supposed or actual racial characteristics. One function of value systems is to legitimate de facto power situations. Therefore, the power situation, including the sources and types of power, becomes relevant to the development and maintenance, or transformation, of systems of race relations. Sources of power vary, but in all societies control over the economy, the means of violence, and the channels of communication constitute major bases of power.

The relation between value systems and power relations is a complex one. On the other hand, the development of the institution of slavery in the Southern states of America and the West Indies, for instance, is not explained by the fact that masters and slaves were physically distinguishable; in the West Indies, African slaves "in significant numbers [were] latecomers fitted into a system already developed."[4] But the physical distinction was a potential source of justification for the institution. The structural basis of economic inequality, in

---

* Many people who are called "immigrants" are even now not immigrants in the strict meaning of the term; however, they are treated as such because of their color.

the case of Negroes, came to be supported by a highly sophisticated value system of racial inequality.[5] Changes in this value system have accompanied changes in the economic relations between black and white, not in the sense of a complete change but in a gradual erosion, with many setbacks, as the economic and power structure changes. It is often claimed that value systems do not exist autonomously from patterns of social relations, but once established and accepted, values do not change mechanically to reflect changed economic and social conditions. The holding of certain values may obstruct or retard economic and social changes. In Britain, for instance, there is no system that separates the people, legally, ideologically, or economically, totally on the basis of their color or ethnic background. Nor is there a system that ignores these characteristics in the allocation of positions within the society in the distribution of jobs, houses, education, as well as prestige and power, or any other scarce resource. Color and ethnic background play some part in differentiating between groups. How do they operate and in which areas of life is their significance increasing? The task is to establish to what extent supposed or real ethnic or race differences affect life chances, and this can only be done if these variables are related in a functional manner to the overall structuring of the social positions of groups and members of groups. To begin to answer such questions we must look at some of the situations in which intergroup relations in Britain are of particular significance. Housing patterns were discussed in Chapter 3. In this chapter some of the developments of inter-ethnic contact in personal relations, education, and employment will be examined.

PERSONAL RELATIONS

Individual sentiments of liking or antipathy are frequently given primacy in discussions of interpersonal contact. Degrees of prejudice and tolerance are used to analyze the extent and type of relationships. Explanations in terms of personality characteristics are comparatively limited because the factors that generate and sustain interpersonal contact are largely social. Robin M. Williams found that if contact opportunities are related to ethnic prejudice and to status-role factors, ". . . the greater differences are associated with the social factors."[6] His studies of minority-majority group contacts in the United States show that four of the main determinants of contact opportunities are sex, age, education, and economic status.[7] Although there are no comparable studies for Britain, where the evidence on interpersonal contact is largely fragmentary and unsystematized, the conclusions from the American data that intergroup contacts are highly patterned and, according to Williams, "interaction a highly predetermined matter" are likely to be equally applicable to the British situation. The main opportunities for interpersonal contact arise at work, in schools or colleges, and in some residential areas. These provide experience from which interpersonal relationships may develop, for instance, among those who have like interests in leisure-time activities. Friendship and intermarriage, as well as the more limited forms of interpersonal contact are possible outcomes of such experience. Despite the diversity of the situations in which interpersonal contacts arise between colored and white and the variations in their form and content, they are not random either in terms of social networks or personality characteristics.* The customary and conventional sanctions prescribing the limits of interaction and the ways in which these are related to hierarchies of power and prestige are a major part of any attempt to account for systematically observed interrelationships.

Studies of intergroup relations in Britain illustrate the influence of the situation on the development and nature of personal interaction. Generally a higher degree of acceptance of

---

* Many studies have used a concept of social distance to document the patterning of attitudes between individuals and groups of different ethnic origins. Emery S. Bogardus developed a scale for measuring social distance as a psychological phenomenon, which, with modifications, has been used for many subsequent studies. Numerous adaptations of the concept over the past thirty years to remedy some of its shortcomings have not been altogether successful. The relationship between expressed attitudes and actual social interaction remains problematic. Furthermore, the evidence of variations in behavior in different social situations focuses attention increasingly upon the relative social positions rather than the personality characteristics of individuals in face-to-face contact.[8]

colored people is found within the work situation than outside it. Peter L. Wright notes that contact is rare except at work. One manager went as far as to claim, "Any friendship between white and coloured ends at the works gate."[9] There were exceptions particularly in the case of West Indians who shared a common interest in cricket or who attended the works' social club. R. B. Davison, in his study of West Indians, records a similar pattern. West Indians reported fairly satisfactory relationships with white people at work but otherwise had little contact. "Very few attend sports meetings, dog or horse racing or bingo sessions." The one "who played in a band, plays skittles, cricket, dances . . . belonged to a social club at the place of work . . ." is described by Davison as the "odd man out" among working-class West Indians.[10]

This lack of contact outside the work situation, other than with family members, is not confined to colored people. Social networks of individuals in urban society tend to be loose knit since there is little overlapping between different areas of social life. In a study of families in cities, Elizabeth Bott has written, ". . . in an urban industrialized society there is no single encapsulating group or institution that mediates between the family and the total society."[11] The separation of work, home, and recreational facilities makes strong interpersonal ties outside the family difficult to achieve.

The conditions under which they arise are therefore fairly specific. Interpersonal contact is a feature of multiracial committees and groups concerned with improving race relations. These are largely confined to small sections of the white middle class and to a few colored people, usually of professional or semi-professional status. (For a discussion of the composition of such groups, see pp. 174–176.) Local groups of British political parties occasionally have colored members and trade union branches in many industries have mixed memberships. The level of activity among colored members is no higher than among the white membership, and contacts are less through regular meetings than at work, or during strike action, or at election times.

Student groups provide a situation in which work and leisure are not separated to the same degree and the way of life is less individuated. This, plus the relative strength of liberal values in many forms of higher education, encourages the inter-mixing of white and colored students. Within the lodging house with mixed tenants proximity also gives rise to oppor-tunities for interpersonal contact that may generate friendly or hostile interaction. Multiracial housing schemes, promoted by a variety of charitable associations to meet housing needs, also provide similar opportunities without the element of ex-ploitation frequently found in the lodging house situation; but the scale of their operations is small. Large numbers of un-attached males in some areas lead to interpersonal contact of a deviant kind. The ready-made market for organized and ama-teur prostitution leads to soliciting by white girls. In a situation where sexual relations between white and colored people are regarded with disfavor and instances of prostitution exist, in-terracial friendships between unattached members of the oppo-site sex are difficult to establish. The pressures against mixed youth clubs in certain areas, for instance, arise, in part, from stereotypes of sexual behavior, but discussion of this problem is largely taboo among those professionally engaged in youth work.

Negative evaluations emerge strongly on the question of in-termarriage—both white and colored have preferred patterns of marriage. The correspondence on this issue in Asian news-papers published in Britain is generally marked by strong dis-approval. Marriage patterns among whites follow class and religious lines in a fairly restricted way. Clearly, in both groups, notions of suitable marriage partners are heavily influenced in favor of those with common experience and background.

At the present time the extent of marriage across color lines, as estimated by local surveys, is small.[12] There are compara-tively few single colored girls of marriageable age compared to the large numbers of colored males. Intermarriage is usually between white girls and colored men. The generation now growing up will experience a different situation. How great the increase in intermarriage will be is difficult to estimate. The chances of intermarriage will be higher to the extent that ex-periences in education, work, and leisure activities come to be shared, but the present imbalance between the sexes within some colored groups will also disappear.

The development of interpersonal relations cannot be accounted for adequately without reference to the developments taking place outside primary group situations. The position of partners in an interracial marriage and the situation of children of mixed parentage vary according to their total socio-economic position. We shall now turn our attention to two areas of particular relevance, education and employment.

EDUCATION AND RELATIONS BETWEEN ETHNIC GROUPS

Education is regarded as having a central role in the development of harmonious ethnic group relations. In Britain it is commonplace to attribute to it a major part in molding relations between the indigenous white and immigrant colored populations. Education, in the sense of transmitting values of tolerance based on a greater understanding and experience of groups of different ethnic origins, is seen by many as the solution to the problems associated with prejudice and discrimination. This transmission involves a two-way process by which colored and white groups evolve a new perception of each other, and the basis of multiracial communities is laid. In this view, intolerance arises from fear and ignorance and so it follows that education is the major way of removing these. In discussing the role of the school, for instance, a prominent researcher and teacher observed that "nothing at the moment is more greatly needed in the world at large and in present-day multi-racial Britain than tolerance, a wise suspension of judgment, and a refusal to be drawn into recrimination, prejudiced action, and above all violence. It is in the multi-racial school that the seeds of tolerance have to be sown."[13]

This makes good sense but needs qualification if we consider the more general relationship of education and social change. There is no fixed, known relationship between them. Social change is a complex process in which education is only one of many variables. It is an oversimplification to attribute to education a dominant role and to ignore other processes within any given situation. The transmission and acceptance of values is not autonomous of the conditions and experiences of everyday life. It is a part of them. Racial intolerance, for instance, does not necessarily rest on ignorance, it can be based on an instrumental assessment of the advantages to be gained from it. Or more simply, but more problematically, it can be accepted as a normal or natural condition of life. In such situations, it is sociologically naïve to assume that education alone will bring about changes in racial attitudes and behavior. It remains only one of many factors in the complex process of socialization and resocialization.

The overall social function of education is to prepare the young for adult life within a given type of society. Within the formal educational system, this involves the interrelated processes of socialization and training. Training is concerned with the imparting and acquisition of skills and techniques that enable the young to fulfill economic and occupational positions. One of the criteria applied to education at all levels, but particularly secondary and higher education, is that of utility. The trend in industrial societies is to give utility a strictly economic and occupational meaning. In this way, the formal educational system can provide the means whereby some of the social and economic disadvantages attached to many of the adult colored population may be removed from the colored children now being educated in Britain. If their employment opportunities can be widened then their allocation in the overall structure of society may approximate more closely to that of white children. This function is directly related to the overall position of colored groups. The socialization function of education transmits values and beliefs not only about education but also concerning many aspects of society. Where conflicts of values exist, the formal system of education can be consistently supporting, transmitting and practicing one set of values, rather than another, to help strengthen these values. The value of racial tolerance is one possible aspect that may be so promoted.

In Britain the content of training and socialization and the degree of emphasis given to one or the other varies with age and ability and the type of institution in which the education is received. Differences occur not only between primary, secondary, and higher education, but within these, according to the dominant social class composition of the school. Education is one of the most crucial means of social mobility, but the educational system itself remains highly stratified. Therefore, children, whether white or colored, receive their education within the context of this stratification, which affects the kind and amount of training they are given and the patterns of values and beliefs to which they are exposed.

The arrival of colored children, coupled with their uneven distribution in schools, led some parents, teachers, and local and national administrators to the view that the problems created by this situation had to be tackled by new administrative and teaching arrangements. Before discussing these arrangements and their effects, certain aspects of the position of the children of colored immigrants and the structure of the British educational system will be briefly viewed.

Children of Migrants

Certain generalizations can be made about this situation, but the differences between and within ethnic groups in terms of their indigenous culture, their socioeconomic position, their attitude toward migration, and their family organization influence the actual experience of the children in a variety of ways. Some of the relevant features of the situation of immigrants and their children were already examined. (See Chapter 3.) Many studies of the children of immigrants in other societies detail these experiences with a richness and depth that bring out the human dilemmas of what sociologists call second-generation problems. Children born or reared in a society different from that of their parents, psychologically and socially, find themselves between two worlds, belonging fully to neither. Concerning children of immigrants to the United States it was said:

> The sons and daughters of the immigrants were really in
> a most uncomfortable position . . . the source of all their
> woes . . . lay in the strange dualism into which they had

been born . . . . whereas in the schoolroom they were too foreign, at home they were too American . . . . How to inhabit two worlds at the same time was the problem of the second generation.[14]

This situation of conflict creates strains and tensions on a personal, family, and community level. It frequently gives rise to crises in behavior, due as much to the opening of new opportunities as to the difficulties of exclusion from the dominant society. The problems that have come to center around the second generation may be much more prolonged than this. To conceptualize the situation as a temporary stage in a necessary, automatic transition toward assimilation or integration is due to the concentration of studies on European immigrants to the United States. Not all immigrant groups become integrated or assimilated even after many generations.[15] Different structural arrangements may and have evolved and persisted over long periods of time. At one end of the scale group, exclusion from the dominant structure may be transitory and insignificant in degree, as with the white Protestants of northwest Europe who went to America, or exclusion may be prolonged and extreme, as with the Negroes in the United States. Furthermore, a similar situation may be experienced by children of mixed parentage who are part of neither community, socially or psychologically. How long and in what situations the problems associated with the second generation continue depends on many factors including the strength of the dominant and minority or immigrant cultures, the mechanisms of social control, the agencies of resocialization, and the degree and kind of exclusion exercised by the dominant society, whether based on religious, ethnic, or color differences.

Children are frequently seen as the agents of social change. For instance, . . . "the assimilative forces which the dominant society exerts upon the ethnic groups are exerted primarily upon the child, so that he rather than the parent becomes the transmitting agent of social change."[16] The child is not, however, the passive recipient of these assimilative forces nor a simple agent of social change. The fabric and tissue of social change is a complex interaction process involving parent-child relationships, the experiences with siblings and other similarly situated peers, the attitudes and behavior of teachers and children within the school, and the experiences outside both the home and school environment, all mediated through the child's perception. In short the degree, rate, and type of social change will depend on the totality of the child's world. When examining the position of colored children in Britain in the context of the British system of education, it is necessary to bear in mind that simple notions of social change, as an inevitable process of assimilation or integration, are insufficient.

The English Educational System

Before any examination of the position of children of colored Commonwealth parents within the educational system can be usefully made, it is necessary to mention briefly some of the major structural features of the system; these are so often ignored when questions about the education of immigrants are discussed. Educational opportunity is closely related to social class. The length of formal education, the type of school, particularly at the secondary level, and the chances of higher education have been examined and their relationship to class background and employment opportunities so frequently demonstrated that it is surprising so little attention has been given to them in discussions of the education of immigrant children.[17] The long term trend has been toward an expansion of educational provision, but little significant redistribution between the different social groups has taken place. Educational expansion has benefited all social groups so that more children from each group now stay at school longer and receive an education that allows them to compete for places in higher education. The proportions from each social group have, however, changed little. Of the manual working-class children, ninety-six out of every one hundred are eliminated from full-time education before the age of seventeen.[18] By the time they are sixteen, 48 percent of the children with an I. Q. of 120+ and 87 percent of those with an I. Q. between 108 and 120 have left school. Those who leave are predominantly from a working-class background.[19] Class chances differ throughout the educational system but become progressively wider throughout school life.

However, if a child from a working-class background does survive beyond seventeen, his academic performance is not greatly different from that of middle-class children. He is still less likely to go on to university, but, if he does, his achievement is similar to that of students from higher class backgrounds.[20]

This relative rigidity of the educational system, despite the general increase in prosperity, the removal of crude economic barriers, and the slowly extending educational provision is not easily or simply explained. The very slight narrowing of class differentials in educational opportunity is much less than was expected from the legislation of 1944. The existence of private education, although varying widely in educational standards, obviously increases the overall chances of middle- and upper-class children. Within the state system, cultural, economic, and social mechanisms still operate against children from manual working-class backgrounds, particularly those of unskilled or semi-skilled levels. Part of the explanation lies in an overall scarcity of educational resources, aggravated by a differential distribution of staff, school buildings, and equipment, both geographically between areas and socially between different types of schools. The practical problems of primary and secondary schools in declining areas have been outlined by the Plowden and Newsome Reports.[21] High teacher turnover, large classes, and inadequate buildings make adequate education a near impossibility. The Newsome Report, after presenting a vivid picture of these problems, goes on to say, "But adequate education in slum areas will always be expensive, more expensive than average. It looks to us as if it has often been less expensive than average, and therefore pitifully inadequate."[22] Such deprivation is not confined to the education available in these areas. Physical and social deprivations are closely related to poor school attainment and children from working-class backgrounds are represented in undue proportions in the below-average group.[23] The obstacles facing staff, parents, and children cannot be tackled successfully in schools or the home without far-reaching changes in the rest of the environment.*

---

* This is not to say that there are no teachers and pupils in such schools who overcome the formidable obstacles presented to them. In

In the case of many children, the situation is further complicated by the gap between the experience of the parents and children and those who administer and teach in the schools. The subtleties of the cultural differences that mark groups of different socioeconomic status are beginning to be recognized and subjected to systematic investigation. The development of adequate teaching techniques is handicapped, to some extent, by the lack of appreciation of how far social experience structures thought and language processes and the relation of these to learning. The implications of Basil Bernstein's work on the gap between English social groups are particularly relevant in this context.[24] Differences in language reflect differences in ways of life in which different world views develop. In this sense the failure of working-class children in secondary education can be related to the lack of congruence between the home background and school environment. The "middle-class values" of the selective secondary school are in many ways antipathetic to the experience of the child in his own community. They reflect differences in educational aspirations, intellectual development, knowledge of and attitudes toward occupational possibilities, as well as differences in language. Many recent investigators have remarked on the processes involved, and some have examined the ways in which these are interrelated to produce a continuing lack of meaningful educational opportunity.[25]

It is against this background of the differential distribution of educational opportunity that the education of children of colored Commonwealth parents must be seen. The likelihood of attending a poorly equipped, inadequately staffed school is

primary education, up to the age of eleven, where the relatively unambiguous acquisition of basic skills of reading, writing, and number work exists, the problem is less acute than in secondary education where no such measurable aims confront the majority of teachers and children. The newly introduced Certificate of Secondary Education seeks to provide such a measurable aim. Examinations and certificates are the easiest and most tangible measure of "success" for a school, but since they imply "failure" as part of the process, they build "failure" into the educational system. This dilemma is increasingly recognized by educationalists and others as a central problem of education.

high for the immigrant child who lives in an area of general social deprivation. The chances of his moving out of such a school is no greater, and probably less, than for a native-born child. Moreover, his problems are increased because he may lack basic language skills, be exposed to conflicting value systems in ethnic as well as class terms, and be aware that education is the royal road to mobility but unable to satisfy his own, his teacher's, or his parents' expectations; his problems are also increased because of the definition of so many of the obstacles he faces as problems of immigrant children, rather than conflicts within the educational system and the wider society. The tendency to look back to some golden age before the colored migrants came is as prevalent in education as it is in housing or employment and as unrealistic.

Racially mixed school populations with differences in cultural backgrounds and language have come to be seen largely as problems. This viewpoint is narrow particularly when, in other parts of the educational system, knowledge of more than one language and culture are considered highly desirable. The approach ignores the positive advantages derived from culturally and racially mixed populations. Cultural differences exist in and between societies and any system of education that aims to develop an awareness of the real world cannot ignore them. There is much to be gained, educationally and otherwise, from experiencing and appreciating cultures other than one's own before fixed ethnocentric attitudes develop. Emphasis on the positive aspects of the present situation in schools is developing slowly and unevenly in Britain but is still counteracted, to a large degree, by the concentration on the problems. Moreover, the problems are treated in innumerable ways as though they were created by and related only to immigrant children.

The response to the arrival of colored children in British schools has varied, but gradually the category of immigrant children has come to be widely used in educational circles. Policies and practices to deal with the problems created by this category have emerged piecemeal and have varied according to local situations and pressures. A recent report, after surveying some of these practices and policies, concluded:

> We believe that positive action must be taken . . . but we equally believe that such action must be based on carefully thought out attitudes . . . . We would point out that many people who work in deprived schools and with the children of immigrants have reported that the work can be stimulating and rewarding and that it offers unique experience in the field of human relations. They talk of the challenge rather than the problem.[26]

The emphasis in this report on positive action is in sharp contrast to other developments that have taken place in the field of education in relation to colored children.

CONCENTRATION AND DISPERSAL. The concentration of these children in particular areas leads to some schools or classes having a predominance of colored children. This is officially regarded as a problem. Before the early and mid-fifties the number of colored children at schools in Britain was infinitesimal. In the days of the British Empire a few children of high-ranking or wealthy parents came from India, the Far East, and to a lesser extent from Africa to receive education at public schools; some still do. Children in the few areas of colored settlement attended their local schools. With the growing numbers of colored immigrants, the situation began to change and in some areas the schools began to have an increasingly mixed racial composition. The total number of children of Pakistani, Indian, or West Indian parents attending schools in Britain is not known. An estimate at the end of 1964 of colored children in England put the figure at 250,000.[27] In January 1966, 1.8 percent of all children in maintained schools, that is, 131,043 children, were classified as immigrants. Among those who were under six years of age, the percentage was 2.4 percent.[28] Whatever the exact figure for colored children born here or elsewhere, the proportion remains very small in relation to the total school population. However, their distribution is uneven due to the patterns of residence discussed in Chapter 3. No borough outside the greater London area had a concentration above 10 percent. Wolverhampton had 10 percent, followed by

Birmingham with 8.7 percent.[29] The distribution between schools, however, may be such that particular ones do have high concentrations.[30]

In June 1965 the Department of Education and Science issued a circular stating, ". . . up to a fifth of immigrant children in any group fit in with reasonable ease, but that, if the proportion goes over about one third either in the school as a whole or in any one class, serious strains arise. It is therefore desirable . . . wherever possible . . . to avoid undue concentrations of immigrant children."[31] There was at that time no official definition of an "immigrant child." Official sanction was in fact given to the dispersal of colored children. Two local authorities had already implemented such a scheme and four other authorities proceeded to do so. One director of education, commenting on the situation in 1966, said that they had been "quite ruthless in cutting down the percentage of immigrant children in schools, and had not taken into account family relationships, which they normally did with local children, allowing brothers and sisters to attend the same school."[32] In other areas, children in the same family are dispersed together. The dispersal scheme has met with opposition from some areas and from some teachers, administrators, and parents of the children concerned. Few asked as one education officer did, ". . . why shouldn't schools in predominantly immigrant areas be predominantly immigrant?"[33] It can be argued that the community character of education is destroyed by the dispersal policy and that the problems of prejudice and discrimination are likely to be exacerbated by such a policy rather than reduced.

No systematic study has been carried out to evaluate the dispersal policy, socially or educationally, as a solution to concentration. It is possible only to comment on some of its consequences. Those who advocate a dispersal scheme do so for a variety of reasons. Some of the most common reasons are as follows: a large concentration of immigrant children in one school or class prevents integration; the parents of white children fear that their children are held back by colored children, particularly those with language problems; children sent to schools in other (predominantly white) areas benefit educationally and the practical problems of teachers in deprived areas are reduced.

The first difficulty was to define an "immigrant child." In some areas, in practice, immigrant means colored; some include children of mixed parentage, others exclude these children. The Department of Education and Science excludes Irish children and children born in Britain whose parents have been in the country ten years. One director of education defined an immigrant child as an immigrant if he constituted "an educational problem."[34] This confusion is not accidental. In a situation where racial prejudice and discrimination are regarded by many as unacceptable, it is necessary to avoid certain terms. Immigrant without any qualifying adjective has come to mean colored, even though the word "colored" is rarely used. This situation is very reminiscent of the debates over immigrants in the early twentieth century when the word Jews was rarely used, but everyone knew what was meant.[35] It is because of this situation that dispersal has become associated with discrimination—whatever its educational value, the wider social consequences cannot be ignored.

For the primary schoolchild, attending a school away from his home area entails practical, psychological, and social problems. Starting school is generally recognized as a stress situation for all children. In the case of a "dispersed" child, this stress is likely to be increased, among other factors, by the longer school day, traveling to a school in a strange environment, and separation from preschool playmates and possibly older siblings. The development of secure psychosocial relationships is hindered because the involvement in a stable environment of home-school relationships is reduced. For instance, after-school activities are restricted, particularly for younger children who live over widely scattered areas. These activities are of particular importance in generally deprived areas.

The position of parents of children who are dispersed raises additional problems. Legally, parents have some choice about what schools their children shall attend. This right is denied to parents of dispersed children.* The practical problems of parents who have young children attending different schools are rarely discussed. The possibilities of developing understanding and cooperation between the parents and teachers are reduced in the very cases where such cooperation is educationally vital, not least because of cultural and language differences. Where the policy applies to colored children only, this differential treatment is not conducive to a reduction in color awareness. Instead, it may well be emphasized in the minds of teachers, children, and parents. As a result of dispersal policies in some areas, the cost of providing transport and, in certain cases, accommodation is high and the increased burden is attributed to the immigrants, not the policies. This factor has been given prominence and has become a political issue, further aggravating relations between colored and white.

The question of concentration and dispersal, seen in the wider perspective of the urban developments of housing and education, becomes a problem not of color but of urban renewal. It is only at this level that a meaningful policy of multiracial housing and educational provision can be pursued.

LANGUAGE AND SEGREGATION. In recent years much attention has been given to the language problem among immigrant children, but research is still at a level where "practical concern outpaces scientific competence."[36] The opportunity for sociolinguistic studies is present in many schools in Britain, but the description of the relevant variables in crucial situations is still awaited in order for the stated aims of educationalists to be put into operation. It is not yet possible to state even in a descriptive way how community and personal beliefs, values, and practices impinge upon the use of language and the acquisition of such use by children.[37] In discussing the interaction of language and social setting, the practical problems of everyday necessarily take precedence over long term research devel-

---

* There has been no test case in this regard. It may be that the circular of the Department of Education and Science is sufficient to justify the action of local authorities. If so, the parents of immigrant children are in a different legal position from other parents.

opments that could provide a more adequate basis for action.

Some of the children of immigrant parents have little or no knowledge of English when they enter schools in Britain. In 1966, 6 percent of immigrant schoolchildren had no English, 19 percent had some English but needed further intensive training, and a further 26 percent had reasonably good spoken English but weak written English. The remaining 49 percent had no problems with their English.[38] The problems faced by teachers of large classes, which included non-English speaking children, led, in some areas, to the setting up of special centers that received newcomers. Such a policy of "integration through separation" involves either special classes attached to "normal" schools or separate centers that cater to immigrants alone. In one school, Spring Grove, work over several years with over 50 percent immigrant children demonstrates what can be done with a particularly interested and acutely aware staff that adopts a flexible approach in developing new methods to deal with the problems that confront the children.[39] The special classes are seen as necessary when large proportions of the children lack a sufficient standard of English to take advantage of ordinary classwork. The emphasis, however, is on the temporary nature of any one child's separation into such classes. As many activities as possible are shared and the children mix freely during play, school meals, school assemblies, and so on. Every effort is made in the school to equip the children for permanent transfer as quickly as possible. With a clear-cut educative purpose of removing linguistic and social handicaps and, at the same time, building a multiracial school, the experiment at Spring Grove appears to have achieved a noteworthy measure of success.

In contrast, the separation of children into separate centers, with perhaps one day a week at a normal school, suffers from educational and social disadvantages. This is particularly so where the schools are staffed predominantly by teachers from the same countries as the children and where the aim of transfer is followed less vigorously. Children in these centers have every encouragement at play, at meals, and so on to speak their own language; they learn little of normal school life and come to regard themselves as separate from the mainstream of educational institutions. The problem is particularly acute for children arriving only a year or two before they are old enough to leave school altogether. For them the educational provision can only be regarded as highly inadequate and the frustration and hostility felt by them and their parents, with the lack of progress in learning even the rudiments of oral English, is frequently blamed on their segregation at school.

Whatever advantages such segregation may have administratively for teachers and normal school populations, its educative advantages for the child are questionable, even for learning a new language. The acquisition of a language is a social process as well as a linguistic exercise. For children who spend any length of time in a segregated center, the social supports and encouragement of building social relationships are diminished and the likelihood of acquiring the necessary language skills are reduced.

THE PROBLEM OF ASSESSMENT. Since our present methods of assessment are inadequate the majority of children of Indian, West Indian, and Pakistani parents are classed as average or below-average, and large numbers of them are classified as educationally subnormal.[40] Some educational difficulties have occurred because of the cultural differences between children from varying ethnic backgrounds. These include the assessment of educational potential and the recognition of the manifestations and causes of disturbed behavior. Unless ways are devised of overcoming these problems, the children from different cultural backgrounds will be at a disadvantage. There are no satisfactory cross-cultural tests; nor is it possible, at present, to isolate the testing of potential from environmentally induced handicaps.[41] From work already carried out the moderate positive correlation between I. Q., for example, and the length of residence and schooling in a western environment among Punjabi boys seems to indicate the important determining role of cultural factors.[42] This is confirmed by a report on the performance of immigrant children in primary schools in the inner London area. Four-fifths of immigrant children were rated below-average but a high proportion were recent arrivals. Performance was positively correlated with length of education in Britain and those who had a full primary education showed no significant differences from other children.[43] This problem of assessment, although most difficult for children arriving in Britain after early experience in their home countries, also affects children born in Britain whose preschool and out of school socialization is within a culturally different environment.

Systematic research is necessary in establishing patterns of disturbed behavior and its typical manifestations in addition to differentiating these from temporary problems of adjustment to a strange environment. Withdrawn or seemingly aggressive behavior may be functionally related to apparently threatening situations. White teachers, relaxed attitudes towards discipline, parental pressure for high-level performance, conflicts of religious beliefs, dispersal to schools outside the child's own area, and, in some cases, delay in entry to schools, particularly where this results from obligatory medical checks for immigrant or colored children, may all serve to put the child in a threatening situation. Initial normal responses to such situations may be attributed quite mistakenly to personality disturbance. Systematic research concerning these and many other problems in the specifically British context is only in its infancy.

Categorization and Race Relations

Whether for administrative convenience or to benefit children thought to have special needs, such as "immigrants," or to avert possible antagonism from indigenous groups, practical steps taken in education on the basis of common sense judgments have developed piecemeal and are not based on a national program of research and continual review.* Such piecemeal practices are institutionalizing differences between children defined as immigrant and nonimmigrant. This process has consequences for social relationships outside the educational system

---

* A circular from the Department of Education and Science states, "It will be helpful if the parents of non-immigrant children can see that practical measures have been taken to deal with the problem in the schools, and that the progress of their own children is not being restricted by the undue pre-occupation of the teaching staff with the linguistic and other difficulties of immigrant children."[44]

and if it becomes accepted as normal that immigrant teachers, immigrant children, and immigrant schools or classes are separate categories, these consequences cannot be other than antipathetic to the development of nonracial attitudes and behavior. Such developments are not consciously designed. They are the result of an empirical approach and a particular ethnocentric definition of the situation. The unofficial but widely used category immigrant teacher, when teachers from India, Pakistan, and the West Indies are referred to, is an instance of this. It is not uncommon for titles such as "Educating the Immigrants" or "Handling the Immigrants: English classes at Smethwick" to appear in educational journals. These are symptomatic of the simplified categorization that lumps together as *the* immigrant people widely differing in ethnic and social backgrounds and ability levels, some with educational problems and some without. One can only speculate as to whether the term "handling" the immigrants is simply an unfortunate word choice or implies a degree of manipulation or control not usually associated with educative processes in present-day Britain. Changing the verbal emphases and definitions of problems is only one step in changing attitudes and behavior. However, a greater awareness is needed of the dangers inherent in continuously using words and phrases that produce a situation in which people come to accept as fact that the immigrant exists who needs "handling." This situation, if allowed to continue or encouraged to develop further by intended or unintended discrimination, is likely to become a self-fulfilling prophecy. The immigrant child will have arrived and intractable problems on the level of race relations will have developed. The following warning could be equally well applied to children described as immigrant in the British educational system: "I can't help feeling wary when I hear anything said about the masses. First you take their faces from 'em by calling them masses, and then you accuse 'em of not having any faces."[45]

When colored children receive their education in schools lacking adequate resources, they are involved in a process of "intensification of disadvantages" shared by all children in such areas.[46] The longstanding problems in British education are not created but highlighted by the presence of colored children.

RELATIONS IN EMPLOYMENT

At the present time the type and grade of work cannot be directly correlated with skin color. In the experience of young colored people now seeking employment, in the difficulties already encountered by colored workers in obtaining promotion, and in the evidence that qualified immigrants are facing undue obstacles in getting work in some nonmanual or professional spheres, there are indications that in the next generation employment will become more clearly related to color. For this to happen, wage and job status differentials between white and colored employees will have to widen but, more especially, there will have to be considerable downward mobility in the case of children of professional colored families and a blocking of upward mobility for working-class colored children. This extreme situation is unlikely. What does appear possible is that jobs offering higher wages, status, and career prospects will become more exclusively the preserve of whites than they already are and colored groups will be increasingly overrepresented in low status, low paid jobs. Discrimination on racial grounds is now illegal. Some discrimination is overt, but as we saw earlier (p. 109) discrimination can be a complex matter interwoven into normal situations. It would be unrealistic to assume that discrimination is automatically eradicated as a consequence of legislation.

Color and Work

For some years the question of color in relation to employment was generally ignored by the majority of those in positions of authority: politicians, local authority officials, employers and trade union officials, and, to some extent, high commission representatives of those countries from which the immigrants came. The official view was that there was no discrimination against colored people. Sporadic complaints were heard from the migrants themselves, but, in the main, their organizations or self-appointed leaders followed a policy of keeping quiet, not causing trouble, and telling members that they must not do anything that would prevent smooth acceptance. Complaints were often attributed to personality difficulties of individuals or it was assumed that any problems were of a temporary nature and that given more time they would disappear.

Personality difficulties exist and in some cases these will be linked with prejudiced attitudes and/or discriminatory behavior (see pp. 106–109). But, for most sociologists, the question to be examined is under what conditions those with personality disturbances *and those without* are encouraged to adopt discriminatory behavior. Group prejudices and patterns of discriminatory behavior are learned social habits and do not disappear "given time." They can, given the right structural setting, increase with time and repetition. Dr. Little in his study of Cardiff's Butetown, published in 1947, advanced the thesis that class and color are related in the minds of the British. Color was associated with the lowest class.[47] Within working-class groups this association may more accurately be regarded as a form of intraclass status consciousness, although for the middle or upper class it may be more straightforwardly class consciousness. Where low status jobs are held by colored workers among the more recent immigrants stereotyping is encouraged, which leads to a more widespread linking of color and low occupational status.

Gradually the complaints came to be accepted as indicative of more than personal individual problems and time was recognized as a possible enemy of nonconflicting race relations, unless positive action was taken. The National Committee for Commonwealth Immigrants held a conference on racial equality in employment during February 1967.[48] Brought together were many government representatives, employers, trade unions, political parties, high commissions, those concerned with "race relations" in a professional capacity, and voluntary bodies, as well as Americans and Canadians dealing in various ways with equality in employment in their own countries. The conference was a recognition that problems exist. One speaker said, ". . . if there had been no discrimination we would not have been having a conference. There has been discrimination and it exists in some very large degree—and we have to face that—and we don't know how to tackle it."[49] In April 1967 a report on racial discrimination presented evidence of widespread discrimination in employment.[50] In October the government announced its intention of introducing legislation to extend the scope of the 1965 Race Relations Act.[51] Only just over a year previously the government's attitude had been that through employment exchanges, youth service, and trade unions, "considerable progress" had been made in solving the problem of immigrant employment.[52] Despite considerable pressure from Labour members of Parliament and immigrant organizations, employment was excluded from the provisions of the 1965 Race Relations Act. During the first two years' work of the Race Relations Board, 309 complaints were received in the first year and of these, 97, the largest number for any single area, related to employment, while in the second year 690 complaints were received, and of the 574 falling outside the act, employment again headed the list with 254 complaints.[53] The various pressures and the increasing evidence of alleged discrimination affected the government's previous attitude. In October 1968 it was made illegal for employers to discriminate in the hiring, promotion, or dismissal of employees, or to discriminate in the conditions of employment on the grounds of color, race, ethnic, or national origins.[54] The act was highly controversial not only for those who oppose any such legislation but for groups concerned with eliminating discrimination by, among other means, legislation. The latter argue that one of the clauses contained in the act, now known as the "racial balance clause," legalizes discrimination, and many have expressed doubts about the adequacy of the arrangements for enforcement of the other clauses in dealing with discrimination in employment.[55] A serious weakness is that complaints relating to employment are dealt with not by the Race Relations Board but by industrial machinery. The actual elimination of discrimination depends not only on the provisions of the act or the means provided for their enforcement but also on the extent to which racial discrimination is recognized when it happens and is followed by appropriate action.

The term "discrimination" is too general to describe and explain relations between white and colored groups within the occupational structure of British society. It lacks the necessary methodological rigor for distinguishing between different types of relationships and leads to confusion of individual behavior, institutional forms, and the structural bases of the differential treatment of groups within industry. Institutionalized patterns of discrimination, for instance, are countered by examples of individual nondiscrimination.* To infer discrimination first it is necessary to have equally qualified people applying for the same jobs in order to isolate color as the only differentiating factor. A colored person competing for a position with a much less well-qualified white is a more straightforward case. Nonetheless, it is part of the relationship of any minority with a dominant group that the possibilities of such competition are minimized not simply by discrimination in job placement but by unequal educational opportunities, training facilities, and the influence of socialization toward appropriate types and grades of work. The bases of discrimination are to be found in a whole range of formally and informally structured situations.

The institutional forms within the employment situation can occur in recruitment, dismissal, training, promotion, and conditions of service. The Political and Economic Planning Report concentrated on recruitment but pointed to the existence of discrimination in dismissal, promotion, pay, and training.[56] The size of the problem is difficult to estimate, because discrimination, other than in a carefully constructed test situation or in a place where there is a declared and acknowledged discriminatory policy, is difficult to prove. Although this is so in recruitment, it is even more the case in promotion, training, and conditions of service. There are situations where it can exist without the people involved realizing it. For instance, one firm that had introduced a pension scheme for its manual grades did not include colored employees in the scheme. The reason given was that the insurance company with whom the scheme

---

* This phenomenon is also very common in the case of women. For instance, individual women in particular high status jobs are used in arguing that general patterns of discrimination do not exist. Equally, the explanation for not employing women in certain types of jobs is that they are unfit temperamentally or biologically for them, that is, in terms of the characteristics ascribed to women, and discrimination is denied.

was arranged refused to include colored workers. As the bulk of these employees were well below pensionable age the situation was not of immediate importance to them nor were they told of the difference in conditions.*

Furthermore, in a situation where discrimination is thought to exist, many colored people do not put themselves willingly into a position where they expect to encounter discrimination. This avoidance pattern is a common means of coping with situations defined as potential areas of conflict, not only in race relations but in other social relations. A schoolteacher from West Pakistan teaching in Britain saw no chance of promotion: "In this country promotion in this field for a coloured person is beyond thinking."[57]

A number of factors have to be examined to determine the relative significance of color in the employment situation. Broadly the employment situation may be defined as the relation between manpower available and the structuring of occupational opportunities. Manpower available depends on a complex of demographic, economic, and social factors of which migration is only one. In Britain, during the period of 1958 to 1963, the time of the agitation and the passing of the Commonwealth Immigration Act, the economy was not overburdened with manpower resources.[58] Nor was it envisaged that the supply of available labor would be increased. "Our manpower resources are expected to grow much more slowly than in recent years."[59] Occupational opportunities are structured by overall economic policy, technological development, and social factors of which race may be one, but others such as education, training, and sex also have to be taken into account.

Recruitment

Opportunities are affected by the policies of managements, officials of employment exchanges, and trade unions who discriminate between potential employees in a number of ways. Some trade unions and employers have agreements that specify con-

---

* Apparently the personnel manager who discussed the situation did not favor the arrangement but could not see what might be done.

ditions relating to the employment of foreign workers. These date back to before or immediately after World War II and were the result of pressure from the unions who feared unemployment or the undercutting of rates and conditions by the use of foreign diluted labor. Such agreements may be applied to colored or Commonwealth workers, although strictly they were devised only for non-British or alien workers. Other collective agreements are concerned with the level of recognized skills. In craft unions the serving of an apprenticeship is the customary method of acquiring such skills.* Many struggles in the past between employers and unions have been over this question of skilled workers and skilled jobs. If they had the power, unions would insist upon skilled craftsmen performing certain tasks at an agreed rate of pay, but employers have redefined work tasks in order to employ those less skilled at lower rates. Those who have not served a British apprenticeship have always faced problems and while some craft unions, particularly with branches overseas, have evolved ways to allow or withold recognition, problems have arisen with craftsmen from the Commonwealth. To what extent these cases have been excuses for discrimination or actually involve unacceptable levels of skill is not known.† Agreements on the number of apprentices to any one craftsman are similarly the outcome of longstanding conflicts between unions and employers centering around the control of the supply of skilled labor and the possibilities of using apprentices as a source of cheap labor. Consequently, the num-

---

* Apprenticeship schemes now operate on an industry and area basis under government training boards. These were set up in an attempt to provide more skilled manpower largely as a result of the N.A.J.C. (National Advisory Joint Council) Working Party on the Manpower Situation. A levy is imposed on employers to encourage more training by individual employers, as well as to finance the government centers. No information is published on the numbers of colored apprentices being trained under the government scheme.

† Cases of nonpromotion to supervisory positions of craftsmen who had not served a British apprenticeship have occurred as the result of union action. When union officials were asked about the nonemployment of colored immigrants in their particular industry or occupation a few attributed this to a color bar by employers, but the most frequent response was "inadequate qualifications and/or training." This applied particularly to craft or nonmanual unions, but one official of a general union gave this reply.[60]

ber, age of entry, and length and conditions of training are formally agreed in many trades. Most colored immigrants were too old on arrival to take apprenticeships, and language difficulties presented a problem in some cases. Because of the crucial part played traditionally by apprenticeship in obtaining skilled status and because of agreement on numbers and preference given to relatives or friends of craftsmen in some trades, entry is restricted. These restrictions affect white as well as colored applicants and girls are virtually excluded. However, the possibility of using the restrictions preferentially on the basis of color remains, and in the future the restrictions may be focused more clearly in this way.

Apart from the special circumstances in skilled trades, the most common allegation of trade unions exercising control over the employment of colored workers arises from the belief that informal agreements exist between them and employers on the quota of colored workers to be employed. Only two employers in the Political and Economic Planning (P.E.P.) survey admitted they used such quotas, and there is no systematic information on the extent of informal quota agreements. However, local cases not only of quotas on numbers to be employed but also on job allocation, promotion, and so on reveal circumstances that appear to be discriminatory. Trade union officials attribute these informal arrangements to pressure from their members in certain branches or firms and each level of official attributes them to a different level of official. The relations between national, regional, and local officials varies formally and in practice between unions and from area to area. In general, at the national level discrimination is condemned in strong terms and resolutions are frequently passed at union conferences against discrimination; in practice, national officials have not gone much beyond this kind of moral pressure although one union, by questioning applicants, attempts to appoint only officials with acceptable views on racial integration. At present, it is possible for unions to ignore or condone racial discrimination and to rationalize in terms of their ignorance of its existence or in terms of the power of the members or of particular officials to continue the practice.

Employers rarely admit officially to operating any form of

color bar. In some industries in fact they clearly acknowledge their dependence on colored workers, although this is sometimes followed by the qualification that if they had a choice they would prefer white labor. Where some form of bar, whether total or on a quota basis, is recognized, it is attributed to a variety of factors. For instance, in one local study, among the reasons given were: "Small labour force"; "not considered advisable to mix nationalities"; or "our type of weaving demands the highest skill and the highest degree of craftsmanship and intelligence as well as a good command of English and spelling. This would preclude Pakistanis."[61] Trade union restrictions or, more diffusely, the attitudes of trade unionists figure quite prominently in reasons given, as well as a belief that objections from employees and customers would arise from the employment of colored workers. The objections may be in terms of the disruptions to on-going relations with other groups in industry or in terms of the real or alleged unsuitability of the colored immigrants themselves. Both sets of factors are used and may be found in combination. Problems do arise for employers from both of these, but both can also be used to discriminate purely on grounds of color. Whether this discrimination is also linked with prejudice is more difficult to determine, but in its consequences this linking is not very relevant. It is the discriminatory behavior that affects job allocation.

Local, regional, and national officials of the Ministry of Labour* are in a position to influence the practices of employment recruiting to some extent. The influence is limited by the numbers of employers and colored people who use their services, the general policy of the Ministry of Labour and the sanctions it has, in addition to the discretion given officials to make interpretations of policy directives. Dr. Davison reported that only 18 percent of the men in his sample obtained their jobs through employment exchanges during the first year and 15 percent during the second. For women the percentages were twenty-six and seven for the first and second years.[62] The P.E.P. survey found about half of those they interviewed had made use of the

---

* The Ministry of Labour is now called the Department of Employment and Productivity.

employment exchange, but only 8 percent had obtained their present job in this way.[63] In the Bradford survey out of 223 Asian men and women interviewed, 60.5 percent had used the employment exchange at one time or another since their arrival in Britain. However, only 10.7 percent had obtained their current job in this way. Similarly, the service is voluntary for employers and overall only a minority of vacancies are notified.[64]

The official attitude of the Ministry of Labour has varied. In the early 1950s it was "one of no discrimination. The principle in placing is suitability for the job, with a preference for local residents."[65] Such a policy might have discriminated against immigrants of any color who could not claim local residence. From the mid-fifties until 1964 there was a departure from no color discrimination, and employers were allowed to specify "no coloreds." The only sanction was that local officials could try to persuade them to change their minds. "It is probably fair to say that more and more 'orders' for workers specify that coloured workers will not be considered."[66] No information on the extent of such "orders" or the procedures used to dissuade them is available. After 1964 it became possible for the services of the Ministry of Labour to be withdrawn from employers who continually discriminated. The effectiveness of this sanction depended on the interpretations of discrimination and the administrative arrangements for its use. It could only be done after referral by a local official to the regional and national officials and to the minister himself. This did not encourage its use. And moreover, the ministry pointed out several reasons, which might be advanced by employers, that could be considered valid in the circumstances of particular cases. Personal prejudice was unacceptable but valid reasons included lack of skill, or belief that certain races were unsuitable for certain kinds of work, or objections from other groups within the industrial situation. Since most employers would present "valid" reasons rather than racial discrimination or prejudice, only a very small minority of cases could fall within the official interpretation of discrimination. Since the 1968 Race Relations Act, recruitment is now formally subject to the changes made by this act; however, the problems of discrimination still remain and evaluation must await empirical studies of the actual processes within employment exchanges.

The attitudes of customers and employees are frequently cited as obstacles to the employment of colored immigrants. There is no systematic information on the attitudes of customers. It appears that when colored people are not employed in stores, banks, or offices, where they would be in contact with the public, one of the explanations given is the problem of customer hostility; however, in many cases, colored employees are found in these positions in other firms or areas without apparently creating hostile customer reaction. Among employees the significance of color appears to be associated more often with the type of work or promotion desired or with questions of dismissal than with barriers to recruitment in general. However, color awareness affects relations within some work situations, although systematic evidence is lacking on the incidence of this or its correlation with other conditions.

When relationships are relatively smooth it is unusual for them to be recorded. Almost all the reports on this matter in national and local newspapers relate to conflict between white and colored workers. These include demands for segregated canteen and toilet facilities, objections to Sikhs wearing turbans, problems concerning overtime working, promotion of colored people, refusal to work particularly with newly recruited colored workers, and so on. Increasingly, since the late fifties, press reports have highlighted the emergence of color awareness and hostility. Some of this is confirmed by studies of the experiences of colored immigrants, but these studies also report a lack of hostility and a more general acceptance than is available from newspaper reporting. For instance, conflicts between Indians and Pakistanis, West Indians and Asians, or even between West Indians from different islands exist. The information, however, is frequently of an anecdotal kind and too unsystematized to be useful for presenting a general pattern. We do not know whether or not the degree of conflict varies with the size of the colored group, although this is widely believed to be the case. Similarly, it is believed that the employment of white women and colored men leads to objections and hostility. The objections may come in this case from white men or the women themselves or it may simply indicate a fear that problems would arise. Studies of differing industrial situations, large and small work groups, mixed and segregated groups in different industries, and different firms will have to be undertaken before myths can be separated from the actual relationships developing within the place of work. At present, avoidance patterns appear to predominate, but this may be due to the selective information available rather than to actual developments. The significance of these selective data lies in the extent to which they are allowed to influence policy and attitudes.

The Distribution of Colored Workers

In 1961 about eight out of every one hundred workers were "immigrants," that is, born outside England and Wales. Of these about two or three out of every hundred are likely to be colored workers.* However, they tend to be concentrated in certain regions, industries, and occupations; so this overall figure is not very useful in understanding either the factors making for the allocation of colored workers within the industrial or occupational structure or the relationships between the white workers, both alien and native, and the colored workers.

West Indians concentrated in London and the Midlands are mostly in transport, on building sites, in a wide range of light industries such as clothing and footwear, food, drink and tobacco, or light engineering and chemicals, or involved in laundries and the nursing profession. Asians in the north and the Midlands are more often found in textile factories, steelworks, engineering, electrical and chemical work, transport, teaching, and medicine. The 1961, 10 percent sample figures show an occupational pattern of concentration of Pakistani men and West Indian men and women in laboring jobs, a position shared with men born in Ireland.[67] A heavy concentration of West Indian women in the professional group is due largely to those

---

* This estimate is based on ministry of pensions and national insurance figures for new entrants to the labor force, and an estimate of the number coming from the "colored" Commonwealth on work vouchers. English-born children are excluded.

who have gone into nursing.* But very few are found in sales or clerical work.

Local studies in various parts of the country, frequently covering a particular immigrant group, show a concentration in unskilled or semi-skilled grades; very few are in white-collar occupations and, from area to area, Pakistanis and Indians are more concentrated in particular industries. In Bradford, for instance, two-thirds of the Pakistanis are in textiles and, within this industry, the Pakistanis are heavily concentrated in combing and spinning. The remaining third, however, are dispersed in a variety of industries such as public transport, foundries, and engineering. Out of a total estimated 8,000 employed in the city, about 1,000 are self-employed or employed in Pakistani businesses, retail shops, laundries, taxi services, restaurants, and so on, serving mainly, but not wholly, the city's colored population. A small proportion are in nonmanual or professional work.[69]

Employment opportunities for non-English speaking unskilled immigrants were largely in the hands of fellow immigrants. In the Bradford survey out of 223 Asians, 42 percent obtained their first job through a relative or friend.[70] Unskilled factory work, as in the textile mills of Yorkshire, short of indigenous labor and having relatively low rates of pay, was open to such immigrants and most of them found jobs of this or a similar kind. Such clustering has important consequences. It produced, in some instances, work groups composed entirely of workers from one ethnic group, organized under one of their

---

* A quarter of all nurses and midwives undergoing training during 1966 were described as immigrants.[68] The nursing profession is regarded as one example of an occupation lacking in racial discrimination. Nonetheless, teaching hospitals, the elite centers for both training and career purposes, have few colored nurses. This may reflect their favorable position in recruitment. They generally take girls of a higher socioeconomic status than other hospitals for training and many have waiting lists. And it may be that when a hospital can be selective, white applicants are preferred; although there is no evidence available on the relative position of colored girls born here, few, as yet, are old enough to enter training, and at least one West Indian (colored) matron has been appointed to a nonteaching hospital. On more than one occasion, she has been asked by an applicant making a telephone inquiry if she objects to colored nurses.

fellow countrymen who spoke English. This led to a number of problems despite its obvious advantages in work organization. Apart from the consequence of segregating the workers so that they had little or no incentive to learn English or adapt to the normal practices of industrial relations, the position of the go-between, in some cases, led to allegations of malpractice. These consisted not only of using bribes to get or retain jobs (which, in some cases, but not all, were payments to kinsmen and not regarded as corrupt by those involved) but also of disregarding agreements on conditions of work or pay. The go-between, or straw boss, was in a relatively privileged position and was unlikely to act as a representative in any trade union sense; he was not primarily concerned with such matters as safety regulations, or extra pay for night or weekend work. Therefore, the onus for protecting such rights fell on the employer. The extent of such behavior is not known, but one consequence was to encourage the belief among employers, trade unionists, and some migrants themselves that immigrants could not be entrusted with supervisory positions.*

The evidence from R. B. Davison's study indicates that the practice of obtaining employment through friends and relatives also applies to English-speaking immigrants.† He found, for instance, that in the first year in Britain 36 percent of the men and 37 percent of the women in his sample secured employment

---

* Some cases of white supervisors exploiting the lack of knowledge of immigrant workers and of taking bribes were reported. These were considered individual failings and not explained in racial terms.

† This practice among recent migrants of securing employment through friends and relatives is frequently commented upon, but rarely is it put into the perspective of practices among the indigenous population. The influence of family and friends, through informal socialization and as an actual means of obtaining a job, obviously varies with class position, and level of skills possessed by the applicant and required in the job. Nonetheless, the interrelationship of kinship and friendship, on the one hand, and occupation, on the other, is not without significance among the indigenous population. The trend in industrial societies toward the separation of occupation from family influences is well known. However, important links remain through socialization and informal relationships in job placement. During an interview by the research team, one employer, the grandson of the firm's founder, who had recently succeeded to his present position on the retirement of his father, complained of the practice among immigrants of getting jobs through relations.[71]

through friends or relatives and these proportions increased in the second year.[72] There is a tendency, therefore, for first-generation immigrants to be confined to jobs or firms already known to their fellow countrymen. It could, and has been, argued that such work is suitable to the qualifications and experience of immigrants, and this is extended to cover many colored immigrants whose qualifications and experiences are very different.

A common method of seeking work is to apply directly to firms known to have vacancies. About a third of those in the studies mentioned obtained jobs in this way. Contact is then not with employment exchange officials or managers at the level of policy-making but with the lower grades of nonmanual workers, clerks, receptionists, and gatekeepers. Individuals in these positions, in spite of their low level in the occupational hierarchy, become, in many situations, key persons in the process of recruitment. One is reminded of Sean O'Casey's comment on being prevented from seeing a recently elevated old friend because, among other things, he had no appointment: ". . . so the little clerks below, by refusing to carry a message, prevented the greater clerk above from carrying out a simple act of Christian charity."[73] The gatekeepers may not be carrying out the policy of the firm, in which case the "official" policy becomes largely irrelevant and inoperative, or they may be carrying out the policy of the superiors in the firm. The following is one example of this kind of practice; a man who was a gatekeeper with the same firm for seven years wrote:

> During my service I had at times between three and ten a day coloured people applying for work and not one of them got past the gate.
>
> On more than a few occasions the people concerned had degrees in engineering and many had worked in engineering for years.
>
> I must make it quite clear that I was working under the instructions of people whose job it was to engage the men.
>
> The excuse given to me was that it was on account of the trade unions as the men would go on strike if any coloured people were employed.

On more than one occasion . . . the men . . . showed me the
adverts for both skilled and unskilled men and they also
knew there were vacancies but not for them because they
were coloured.[74]

The attitudes of employers was commented upon as early as
1954 by the General Secretary of the Ministry of Labour Staff
Association:

Some employers, when first offered coloured workers, refuse at once. Many are willing to employ a few because
they need workers badly. A fair proportion later refuse to
take on more or severly limit the numbers. One bad experience will turn an employer against coloured workers;
others really prefer local labour or fear that trouble will
arise if the proportion of coloured to white workers rises
too high.[75]

The situation in which the behavior of one individual belonging to an ethnic community is generalized to the whole group
and then used to represent all members of the group is one of
the commonest forms of discrimination rationalized in terms of
personal experience. The ambiguities in both the situation and
the attitudes is illustrated by the reply of one textile firm employing mainly women: "We have had only one Pakistani girl
work for us. The result was not very encouraging—poor time
keeping and no appreciation of quality or pace. However, we
have even seen such signs in British workers."[76] Such an approach is inherently discriminatory but has not developed into
the full-fledged stereotyping of "We do not employ West Indian
women because they have stubby fingers, not suitable for our
branch of textiles."[77]

The lack of skills of some first-generation immigrants in
addition to their language problems and cultural differences
are generally accepted as genuine reasons for restricting the
opportunities open to these people. The evidence in the P.E.P.
survey and other surveys indicate two important aspects of this.
First, the tendency to use such arguments for all colored immigrants, regardless of language and occupational skill, and
second, the extension of this discrimination to the second gen-

eration, where color becomes the most important distinguishing characteristic, makes widespread discrimination acceptable.

Color and Skill Recognition

Since the introduction of work vouchers and the subsequent tightening of the regulations in 1965, the composition of immigrant groups has become polarized in skill and educational terms. Of those entering before 1962 there was a high proportion of unskilled or semi-skilled, some of whom were illiterate in their own language and knew little or no English. Since 1965 only those with special qualifications can obtain work vouchers and, in potential occupational terms, constitute a professional and white-collar elite.* It is to a large extent the experience of this group and the small proportion of those who entered earlier with similar qualifications that has highlighted the problems experienced in employment by colored people.

Although the illiterate and unskilled immigrants are in some senses the most vulnerable and the most segregated, they are also in a situation that protects them from encountering the kinds of discrimination in employment experienced by others. The English-speaking immigrant with varying degrees of manual skills and the nonmanual and semi-professional immigrants, while having a somewhat wider range of occupational opportunity, are, at the same time, more likely to encounter problems because of their color. There is little agreement on whether colored people seeking work in Britain experience an up- or downgrading in terms of skill and educational level.[78] The discrepancies are due to variations and difficulties in collecting information, the objective problems of comparability of skills, and the part played by personal assessment of applicants and employers. These factors are so intricately interwoven in the whole process that producing a clear and undisputed account of the present situation is an extremely difficult task. To assign weights to the part played by any of these factors is an even more hazardous undertaking. And yet the question of how far

---

* Many immigrants coming to Britain from Kenya are likely to be in this group.

color is affecting the distribution of jobs is basic to the developing pattern of race relations. Whether or not those with skills and educational qualifications are getting jobs or promotion commensurate with their qualifications and perhaps, more especially, whether children born and educated in Britain will be able to compete on equal terms with those of the same age and educational level, regardless of color, are questions that cannot be left unexamined.

It is not difficult to find evidence in Britain of individuals possessing skills who have experienced problems in getting work at a level comparable to their skill. The Political and Economic Planning Report and my own research reveals this as a significant problem area.[79]* It is significant in two senses. First, the explanations given for not employing colored people or employing them only in unskilled or semi-skilled work are usually not color but the fact that they speak English poorly, or not at all, and obtained only a low level of skill in their country of origin, and the problems created by wide cultural differences that exist between Indians, West Indians, and Pakistanis, on the one hand, and the English (white) employees, on the other. The group who fit such a description most closely made the fewest claims of discrimination in the Political and Economic Planning Report; but "immigrant claims were particularly high among those with English trade and professional qualifications."[80] Those who argue that when the colored minorities have opportunities for acquiring skills, learning the language, and divesting themselves of their ignorance of English cultural habits, all will be well, have little to gain by way of support from examining the current evidence. Second, this attitude is significant because it reveals some of the formal and informal social processes that militate against equal treatment. In some cases a process of redefining skills is taking place where col-

---

* At the beginning of my research project this problem was not specifically marked out for investigation. It emerged within the first few months as a major source of difficulty for first-generation immigrants with qualifications. Careful recording of cases was undertaken, work on comparability of qualifications was begun, together with systematic observation of variations in experience in Britain between different professional groups.

ored applicants are involved and a higher or more general level of skills is demanded from them than from the white applicants. Those with qualifications based on education, training, or experience for higher grade occupations still constitute only a small proportion of colored workers in Britain. Their experience indicates, however, some of the problems that second-generation colored people may well face.

In professional groups, as well as in trade unions, employers' organizations, and local and national government departments, variations in the organization, particularly in the system of control and decision making, influence the pattern of recruitment. Personal prejudice has to be seen in this context and is only one element in determining the degree to which racial discrimination will be encouraged or discouraged in recruiting in a wide variety of occupations.

Blanket denials of discrimination, such as that made by the National Union of Teachers, indicate refusal to recognize the existence of any problem:

> The Department of Education is anxious not to reject suitable persons who could help in our present teacher shortage. The local education authorities, some of them desperately short of qualified teachers, would not willingly turn away one single teacher whom they believe to be capable of doing the professional job that a teacher is required to do. Equally, the Union and its members individually are most anxious to welcome, and to help, their colleagues from overseas to find suitable employment in this country. The Union is satisfied that there is no racial discrimination in the field of education.[81]

No evidence was produced by the National Union of Teachers to substantiate its claim. The allegations of institutional discrimination in the formulation of rules and the administration of them are countered by reference to individual teachers who are employed: "We know of many excellent teachers who are making a very valuable contribution to the work in our schools."[82] There is also some evidence that Asian doctors are found mainly outside teaching hospitals and overrepresented at the lower levels of hospital medical hierarchies, but underrepresented in general practice and in higher positions of the hospital service. Until studies are made of the relationships between colored and white colleagues within professional work situations, statements like that of the National Union of Teachers must be treated as expressions of official ideologies and not as analyses of what actually takes place within the professions.[83]

Unemployment

One stereotype relating to colored people is that they come to this country not to work but to live off the welfare state to which they have not contributed. This is not borne out by the information relating to the level of economic activity of immigrants as compared to the native-born. It shows a higher level for those from the colored Commonwealth (except for Pakistani women) than among the native-born population. (See Tables 6A and 7A in Appendix.) At the time of the 1961 Census the analysis of information for twenty-eight London boroughs revealed that while 66 percent of the men born in England were "economically active," the percentage for men born in the colored Commonwealth was between 10 to 20 percent higher.[84] (See Table 8A in Appendix.) However, the statistical information on national and local unemployment is deficient in many respects. For instance, we cannot know the rate of unemployment of colored workers since we do not know the totals employed. Moreover, since 1962 the statistics collected by the Ministry of Labour have been in terms of country of origin and therefore do not separate colored from white. Figures for local areas in the months before and immediately after the imposition of controls on immigration showed colored immigrants to be disproportionately represented among the unemployed.[85] These figures were associated with the rapid increase in immigration, and a response to the threat of control, coupled with a slight recession in 1962 in some areas. As the new arrivals found work the figures dropped rapidly. Table 6 shows that for most of that time the unemployed Commonwealth immigrants as a percentage of the total number unemployed has remained relatively stable.

Table 6. *Unemployed Commonwealth Immigrants as a
Percentage of Total Adult Unemployed*

	1962	1963	1964	1965	1966	1967	1968
January	–	4.9	4.0	2.4	2.4	2.8	2.8
April	–	5.6	3.3	2.5	2.4	3.1	–
July	10.0	4.5	2.8	2.4	2.5	3.3	–
October	6.6	3.8	2.5	2.4	2.2	3.1	–

SOURCE: Report of the Race Relations Board for 1967–68 (London: H.M.S.O., May 28, 1968), p. 53. Reproduced by permission.

In general terms colored workers are not experiencing disproportionately high levels of unemployment.* However, the situation in some local areas is less reassuring. In Bradford during February 1967, for instance, immigrants accounted for nearly a quarter of the unemployed.[87] Although these were not long-term unemployed, immigrants, who make up somewhere in the region of 8 to 10 percent of the work force, were clearly over-represented. Caution is necessary in interpreting this, as the industries in the area hardest hit by the economic recession were those in which the immigrants were most heavily concentrated.

An inevitable worsening of race relations is frequently believed to be associated with increases in unemployment. Evi-

---

* The Ministry of Labour investigations into the characteristics of the unemployed showed that in August 1961, out of a total of 219,000 males and females, aged over eighteen and wholly unemployed, only 5,000 were considered difficult to place on grounds of color. In October 1964, out of a total of 313,000 wholly unemployed males and females, there were 3,300 considered difficult to place for the same reason and 1,040 because of the inability to speak English. A further 5,110 had qualifications but their experience or skill was not acceptable to employers.[86] These figures relate only to the months of August 1961 and October 1964 and the reasons for unemployment are based on assessments by local officials. The fact that the category of color appears at all is an indication that the problem is recognized, but it would be unwise to read more than this into the figures because of variations in assessments. A number of colored unemployed are likely to be included in the categories of inability to speak English and unsuitable qualifications, as well as all the other categories, but there is no indication of how many. The majority of those unemployed and difficult to place because of color in October 1964 had been out of work for less than one year.

dence is cited from other societies linking economic depression with outbreaks of racial conflict, and the recent manifestations of racial stereotyping and demonstrations in Britain have been interpreted as symptomatic of economic decline. In a general sense, economic recessions, or the belief that an overall economic decline exists, are potential situations in which to seek scapegoats to account for real or alleged economic ills.* Minority group members are convenient targets. This process may lead not only to an increase in racial awareness but also to attempts to replace workers of minority group status with workers from the dominant group. In this way, unemployment may rise rapidly among colored workers which, in turn, appears to substantiate the view that they do not work anyway. However, the relation between economic organization and racial conflict is oversimplified, if it is assumed that the process is inevitable.

With a very high rate of national unemployment, such a process is more likely to occur than if the overall rate is generally low. Moreover, if unemployment tends to be localized to certain areas or certain industries, it depends on which jobs and in what areas colored workers are found. Nationally, unemployment in Britain since World War II has been low and localized and colored workers, in general, have gone to industries and areas where there are labor shortages.[89] Single males are also more mobile, so they are in a position to move to other areas if they lose their jobs.

Only where colored and white workers are competing for the same jobs, within the same industry and area, is there a possibility that discrimination on racial grounds will be increasingly practiced in a situation of rising unemployment. Although white workers, employers, and trade unions, for example, may favor a policy of colored workers being laid off first, it is only

---

* In April 1968 the speech of Enoch Powell (member of Parliament) was widely interpreted as linking colored immigrants with problems both social and economic. The *Daily Telegraph* (April 24, 1968) reported 97 percent of the letters it had received on the race issue supported Powell. Typical of many comments was ". . . let it be acknowledged that he [Powell] spoke the language of truth recognised as such by the great majority of our people."[88]

possible for them to follow through with such a policy under certain circumstances. In so far as colored workers are found in jobs that white workers have left, as opportunities for better wages and conditions have been open to them, white workers may prefer unemployment with wage-related benefits instead of what they consider to be low paid, low status jobs. White workers, in other words, have to be willing to compete with colored workers in the same areas, industries, and skill levels. What applies across industries and areas applies within firms and organizations. For instance, in woolen textiles there has developed a system of job allocation in which white workers predominate in certain processes and colored workers in other processes. The two groups are interdependent in the overall functioning of the production process. To dismiss the Pakistanis would leave the white workers without processed wool to work on. The degree of interdependence arising from pluralistic activities is significant in a wide range of industries. A general reorganization of the work force is possible in order to follow a racially discriminatory layoff policy, but such a course is likely in situations of long-term general unemployment rather than in short-term localized unemployment. Where complete substitutability exists between white and colored workers, where no differences of skills, wages, or conditions are found, then the dismissal of colored workers is a practicable proposition.

FUTURE TRENDS

Already the structuring of intergroup relations owes much to the problems and rigidities of traditional British society. In education we saw how certain processes designed to fit the English system have led to the categorizing of children along color lines. Similarly, the employment situation is crucially affecting the development of white-colored relations. In so far as employment is directly related to the other variables of stratification, so the allocation to occupations along the lines of color influences relative positions within the overall stratification system. Standards of living, hierarchies of prestige and power are all associated with the type and level of occupation. In the normal process, the poorer, less articulate, and less skilled are relegated to the bottom of the occupational ladder, whatever their color. But because a disproportionate number of colored immigrants fall into this category, their joining of the under-privileged sections of British society is consequential for race relations. On the one hand, it leads to stereotyping of colored groups as suitable only for certain types of work and accustomed to low standards of living. On the other hand, it encourages the belief among colored people that they are invariably discriminated against in occupational terms, which is reinforced by the experience of those qualified immigrants who find themselves in low paid, low-grade work because of their color. Young colored people including some graduates of British universities are increasingly affected by these processes. The occupations that they achieve will be indicative of how far stereotyping and discrimination are to mark the relations between white and colored not only in employment, but also more generally, and how far color will be less relevant than qualifications.

The present situation demonstrates, to a certain extent, the observation made by Glazer and Moynihan that "It is only the experience of the strange and the foreign that teaches us how provincial we are."[90] The question is whether the recent experience of colored immigration will lead to greater provincialism or whether, through the sharing of common experiences, ties will be forged across the boundaries of color. Some aspects of this question are discussed in Chapter 5.

Notes

1 W. G. Sumner, *Folkways* (Boston: Ginn, 1906), p. 13.

2 T. W. Adorno et al., *The Authoritarian Personality* (New York: Harper & Row, 1950).

3 Tamotsu Shibutani and Kian M. Kwan, *Ethnic Stratification: A Comparative Approach* (New York: © Copyright, THE MACMILLAN COMPANY, 1965), pp. 17–18. Reproduced by permission.

4 U. B. Phillips, *Life and Labor in the Old South* (Boston: Little, Brown, 1929), p. 25.

[5] For a discussion of the relation of economics to ideology and politics of the slaveholding South, see Eugene D. Genovese, *The Political Economy of Slavery: Studies in the Economy and Society of the Slave South* (New York: Pantheon, 1966).

[6] Robin M. Williams, Jr., *Strangers Next Door, Ethnic Relations in American Communities* (Englewood Cliffs, N.J.: Prentice-Hall, 1964), p. 157.

[7] *Ibid.*, pp. 144–156.

[8] Emery S. Bogardus, "Measuring Social Distance," *Sociology and Social Research* (September 1925), pp. 299–308; Bogardus, "Changes in Racial Distance," *International Journal of Opinion and Attitude Research*, 1, no. 4 (1957), 55–62.

[9] Peter L. Wright, *The Coloured Worker in British Industry* (London: Oxford University Press, 1968), p. 184.

[10] R. B. Davison, *Black British* (London: Oxford University Press, 1966), p. 135.

[11] Elizabeth Bott, *Family and Social Network* (London: Tavistock, 1957), p. 100.

[12] See Clifford S. Hill, *How Colour Prejudiced Is Britain?* (London: Gollancz, 1965), p. 222.

[13] June Derrick, "School—The Meeting Point," in Robin Oakley (ed.), *New Backgrounds,* published for the Institute of Race Relations (London: Oxford University Press, © Institute of Race Relations, 1968), p. 135. Reproduced by permission.

[14] M. L. Hansen, "The Problem of the Third Generation Immigrant," in J. A. Jackson, *The Irish in Britain* (London: Routledge and Kegan Paul, 1963), p. 160.

[15] For a discussion of degrees and processes of absorption, see S. N. Eisenstadt, *The Absorption of Immigrants* (London: Routledge and Kegan Paul, 1954).

[16] W. L. Warner, *Structure of American Life* (Edinburgh: Edinburgh University Press, 1952), p. 126.

[17] See A. H. Halsey, J. Floud, and Anderson, *Education, Economy and Society* (Glencoe, Illinois: Free Press, 1961); *Fifteen to Eighteen,* Crowther Report, Vols. 1 and 2 (London: H.M.S.O. Central Advisory Council for Education, 1959 and 1960); *Half Our Future,* The Newsome Report (London: H.M.S.O., 1963); *Early Leaving* (London: H.M.S.O., Central Advisory Council for Education, 1954).

[18] A. Little and J. Westergaard, "The Trend of Class Differentials in Educational Opportunity in England and Wales," *British Journal of Sociology*, 15, no. 4 (1964), 306.

[19] B. Jackson and Dennis Marsden, *Education and the Working Class* (Baltimore: Penguin, 1966), p. 231.

[20] J. G. H. Newfield, "Some Factors Related to the Academic Performance of British University Students," *Sociological Review*, Special Monographs no. 7 (October 1963).

[21] *Half Our Future, op. cit.; Children and Their Primary Schools: A Report of the Central Advisory Council for Education*, The Plowden Report (London: H.M.S.O., 1967).

[22] *Half Our Future, op. cit.*, p. 26.

[23] *Ibid.*, pp. 15–16.

[24] B. Bernstein, "Social Class and Linguistic Development," in Halsey, *op. cit.*, Chapter 24.

[25] See Jackson and Marsden, *op. cit.*, and J. W. B. Douglas, *The Home and The School* (London: MacGibbon and Kee, 1964).

[26] "Children in a Changing Community," *A report by the Joint Subcommittee of the Brent Teachers' Association and the Willesden and Brent Friendship Council*, mimeographed, 1968. Reproduced by permission.

[27] R. J. Goldman and F. M. Taylor, "Coloured Immigrant Children: A Survey of Research Studies and Literature on Their Educational Problems and Potential in Britain," *Educational Research*, 8, no. 3 (June 1966), 164.

[28] *Report of the Race Relations Board for 1967–68* (London: H.M.S.O., May 28, 1968), p. 46. Of the total, 43.7 percent came from the West Indies, 18.6 percent from India, and 6.0 percent from Pakistan. Children born in Britain whose parents have been here for a ten-year period and children of mixed parentage are not included.

[29] In boroughs with populations of 100,000 or over, where immigrant children are more than 2 percent of the school population, the highest concentration is 23.1 percent, followed by 22.6 percent, and 21.3 percent. All three are in the greater London area (*Ibid.*).

[30] In Birmingham in 1965, twenty-two primary schools had between 16 percent and 70 percent. Goldman and Taylor, *op. cit.*, p. 167.

[31] "The Education of Immigrants," *Department of Education and Science, Circular 7/65* (London: H.M.S.O., June 1965), p. 2. Reproduced by permission.

[32] T. F. Davies, "Administrative Problems in Bradford," *Report on The Immigrant Child and The Teacher* (Race Relations Com-

mittee of the Religious Society of Friends, April 1966), p. 16. Reproduced by permission.

[33] Reproduced from the *Times Educational Supplement*, May 3, 1968 by permission.

[34] Davies, *op. cit.*, p. 16.

[35] See John A Garrard, "Parallels of Protest: English Reactions to Jewish and Commonwealth Immigration," *Race*, 9, no. 1 (July 1967), 47–66.

[36] Dell Hymes, "Models of the Interaction of Language and Social Settings," *Journal of Social Issues*, 23, no. 2 (April 1967), 8.

[37] *Ibid.*

[38] *The Report of the Race Relations Board for 1967–68, op. cit.*, p. 46.

[39] Trevor Burgin and Patricia Edson, *Spring Grove, The Education of Immigrant Children* (London: Oxford University Press, 1967).

[40] R. J. Goldman, "The Present Position Relating to Education and the Racial Situation in Britain," Background Paper, *Second Annual Race Relations Conference* (London: Institute of Race Relations, Royal Anthropological Institute, and British Sociological Association, September 1967). Dr. Goldman's own hypothesis is that these imigrant groups on the whole tend to be above-average in intelligence and drive because they have had the initiative to move from poverty-stricken and depressed areas.

[41] Goldman and Taylor, *op. cit.*, pp. 171–173.

[42] C. K. Saint, "Scholastic and Sociological Adjustment Problems in the Punjabi-speaking Children in Smethwick" (unpublished M. Ed. dissertation, University of Birmingham, 1963).

[43] "The Education of Immigrant Pupils in Primary Schools," Inner London Education Authority Report, no. ILEA 959 (December 1967), in *Report of the Race Relations Board for 1967–68, op. cit.*, p. 46.

[44] *Department of Education and Science, op. cit.*

[45] J. B. Priestley, *Saturn Over the Water* (London: William Heinemann, 1961), p. 71.

[46] For a discussion of this process as it affects children in primary schools, see Douglas, *op. cit.*, pp. 31–51, pp. 101–128.

[47] K. Little, *Negroes in Britain: a Study of Racial Relations in English Society* (London: Routledge and Kegan Paul, 1948).

[48] "Racial Equality in Employment" (London: National Committee for Commonwealth Immigrants, 1967).

49 *Ibid.*, p. 98.

50 *Report on Racial Discrimination* (London: Political and Economic Planning, 1967), Section II Employment, pp. 19–68.

51 Report on the Queen's Speech, *Times,* October 31, 1967.

52 "Immigration From the Commonwealth," Cmnd. 2739 (London: H.M.S.O., August 1965).

53 *Report of the Race Relations Board for 1966–67* (London: H.M.S.O., April 1967), p. 18; *Report of the Race Relations Board for 1967–68, op. cit.,* p. 33.

54 *Race Relations Act 1968,* Chapter 71 (London: H.M.S.O., 1968).

55 *Ibid.,* Clause 8, section 2 reads:
"It shall not be unlawful by virtue of either of these sections to discriminate against any person with respect to the engagement for employment in, or the selection for work within, an undertaking or part of an undertaking if the act is done in good faith for the purpose of securing or preserving a reasonable balance of persons of different racial groups employed in the undertaking of that part as the case may be."
In section 4 of the same clause racial group is defined in relation to clause 8 as ". . . a group of persons defined by reference to colour, race or ethnic or national origins and for the purposes of that subsection persons wholly or mainly educated in Great Britain shall be treated as members of the same racial groups."
Clause 3 defines "reasonable" in terms of all the circumstances but particularly the "proportion of persons employed in those groups" and the extent "to which the employer engages, with respect to employment . . . in discrimination of any kind which is unlawful by virtue of this Part of this Act."

56 *Report on Racial Discrimination, op. cit.,* pp. 19–68.

57 Sheila Allen, "Employment Situation of Commonwealth Immigrants within the Industrial Structure of Bradford," Research Report (Bradford: University of Bradford, 1966–69).

58 "The Pattern of the Future," Manpower Studies, no. 1 (London: H.M.S.O., Ministry of Labour, 1964), p. 7.

59 *Ibid.,* p. 7. The contrast in this respect between the European countries and the United States was pointed out: "Over the next decade the rate of increase expected in the U.S.A. is more than four times that expected in this country and in the E.E.C. [European Economic Community] countries" (*Ibid.,* p. 8).

60 S. Allen and J. Bornat, "Trade Unionism among Commonwealth Immigrants in Bradford," mimeographed (University of Bradford, February 1968), pp. 11–12.

61 "Immigrant Project," mimeographed (Keighley Junior Chamber of Commerce, n.d.), p. 6.

62 Davison, *op cit.*, p. 78.

63 W. W. Daniel, *Racial Discrimination in England,* based on the Political and Economic Planning Report (Baltimore: Penguin, 1968), p. 141.

64 *Ministry of Labour Gazette,* 76, no. 5 (May 1968), p. 391.

65 Emrys M. Thomas, "West Indian Workers," *Socialist Commentary,* 18 (December 1954), p. 357.

66 *Ibid.*

67 Since the 10 percent sample is divided according to birthplace rather than color, this may account for some of the discrepancy between the percentage of those born in India working in clerical, professional, and administrative jobs compared to the population as a whole (35 percent as against 18.9 percent). It has also been suggested that Indians may have upgraded their jobs more than other groups. (Davison, *op. cit.*, p. 69.) It is difficult to see why this should be so, particularly in relation to Pakistanis who have many of the same pressures to upgrade their jobs. The low figure of laborers, 6.7 percent of those born in India, is likely to be an underestimate.

68 *Report of the Race Relations Board for 1967–68, op. cit.*, p. 59.

69 Studies relating to employment within local areas include: Davison, *op. cit.;* F. J. Bayliss and J. B. Coates, "West Indians at Work in Nottingham," *Race,* 7, no. 2 (1965), 157–166; Roger Bell, *Supplement to Institute of Race Relations Newsletter,* September 1966; John Goodall, *Supplement to Institute of Race Relations Newsletter,* October 1966; Daniel Lawrence, *Supplement to Institute of Race Relations Newsletter,* June 1966; Rashmi Desai, *Indian Immigrants in Britain,* published for the Institute of Race Relations (London: Oxford University Press, © Institute of Race Relations, 1963); Wright, *op. cit.;* Sheila Patterson, *Dark Strangers* (London: Tavistock, 1963) and Sheila Patterson, *Immigrants in Industry* (London: Oxford University Press, 1968); Sheila Allen, *op. cit.*

70 For other examples of relatives' help in obtaining jobs for the immigrant, see Desai, *op. cit.*, pp. 78–82.

71 See M. P. Carter, *Home School and Work* (New York: Pergamon Press, 1962); E. T. Keil et. al., "Youth and Work: Problems and Perspectives," *Sociological Review,* Vol. 14, no. 2 (July 1966).

72 Davison, *op. cit.*, p. 78.

[73] Sean O'Casey, *Autobiographies*, Volume II (London: Macmillan, 1963), p. 65.

[74] Letter in the *Bradford Telegraph & Argus*, December 19, 1967. Reproduced by permission.

[75] Thomas, *op. cit.*, p. 357.

[76] "Immigrant Project," Keighley Junior Chamber of Commerce, *op. cit.*, p. 7.

[77] Interview with research team, "Employment Situation of Commonwealth Immigrants Within the Industrial Structure of Bradford," *op. cit.*

[78] One survey carried out in 1961 showed that the skill level of immigrants in skilled and semi-skilled work in Britain had risen since their arrival (Economist Intelligence Unit, *Studies of Immigration from the Commonwealth*, 4, London 1962–3, p. 9). Among 236 male West Indians in London, 54 percent had a lower level and only 5 percent had a higher one (Glass, *Newcomers: The West Indians in London* [London: G. Allen and Unwin, 1960], p. 31). The Political and Economic Planning Survey found only 7 percent of nonmanual immigrants were occupied on a comparable level after arrival in Britain and 50 percent of nonmanual immigrants were in unskilled work. Of those with manual skills two-thirds remained on the same level (*Report on Racial Discrimination, op. cit.*, pp. 19–20). My own research shows a similar downgrading of those with nonmanual skills and more continuity of those with manual skills. Because of the incomparability of skill levels between industrial and agricultural employment it is misleading in many cases to claim a rise in skill where immigrants have moved into machine-minding in factories from peasant farming. The official view in 1962 was that ". . . relatively few of them [Commonwealth immigrants] possess any high degree of skill . . ." (National Joint Advisory Council Report on Manpower Situation, *Ministry of Labour Gazette*, Vol. 70, no. 2, February 1962).

[79] See *Report on Racial Discrimination, op. cit.*, pp. 23–26, pp. 32–33.

[80] *Report on Racial Discrimination, op. cit.*, p. 33.

[81] *The National Union of Teachers Views on The Education of Immigrants* (London: National Union of Teachers, January 1967), p. 14. Reproduced by permission.

[82] *Ibid.*, p. 14.

[83] For instance, one case documented was of a Sikh with "qualified status" from the Department of Education and Science who had

made fifty such applications. He was told in writing by more than one authority that his English was not good enough. They had not spoken to him nor he to them. One authority who had refused him a job because there were no vacancies closed down classes in the schools a few months later because of lack of teachers. There are many others who experienced similar situations.

A letter to *The Guardian*, March 12, 1965, cites cases of two Indians, one a lawyer and the other an engineer, both British trained, who had not succeeded in getting employment commensurate with their qualifications.

[84] Davison, *op. cit.*, p. 68.

[85] See Davison, *op. cit.*, p. 89 Table 43; Goodall, *op. cit.*; E. Butterworth (ed.), *Immigrants in West Yorkshire* (London: Institute of Race Relations, 1967), pp. 32–41.

[86] See *Ministry of Labour Gazette*, 70, no. 4 (London: H.M.S.O., April 1962), 133 and *Ministry of Labour Gazette*, 74, no. 4 (London: H.M.S.O., April 1966), 157.

[87] Butterworth, *op. cit.*, p. 32.

[88] *The Guardian*, April 24, 1968. Reproduced by permission.

[89] Statistics collected by the Ministry of Labour show that between 1954 and March 1968 the monthly adjusted averages for wholly unemployed males and females, excluding former students as a percentage of total employees, never rose above 2.4 percent in any one month. Regional variations can be seen in the table on p. 161.

[90] Nathan Glazer and D. P. Moynihan, *Beyond the Melting Pot* (Cambridge, Massachusetts: The M.I.T. and Harvard University Press, 1963), p. 14.

Highest and Lowest Monthly Rates of Wholly Unemployed
Males and Females Over the Period 1954–68

| Region | UNEMPLOYMENT RATES SEASONALLY ADJUSTED | |
	Highest	Lowest
London and South East*	1.7	0.7
Eastern and Southern*	1.9	0.8
West Midlands	2.0	0.4
East Midlands	1.8	0.8
Yorkshire and Humberside*	2.3	0.9
South West	2.6	1.1
North West	2.7	1.0
Northern	4.3	1.4
Scotland	4.4	2.2
Wales	4.2	1.7

* From 1965 only.

SOURCE: *Ministry of Labour Gazette,* 76, no. 4 (London: H.M.S.O., April 1968), 321–330, based on Tables 107–116. Reproduced by permission of the Controller of Her Majesty's Stationery Office.

Chapter 5 ◉ A Society in Transition

In examining the position and treatment of colored minorities now living in Britain, it is necessary to avoid distortion or idealization of the complex reality of social events and relationships by using a simple structural explanation and it is also necessary to avoid the assumption that a total description of events and relationships is possible. Some degree of abstraction from reality is an inevitable process in all sociological, indeed, in all scientific procedures, and this involves a differential emphasis on the aspects that are isolated from the totality. The sociologist, in selecting what he understands to be the more significant features of the structure, must give recognition to the "experienced reality" of the groups and individuals involved in particular situations.[1]

Colored minorities have been seen as an integral part of the changing structure of British society and some specific relationships and situations have been discussed in detail. It is possible to characterize their position within this context in terms of three sets of major influences: the immigrant-indigenous situation, the colonial-metropolitan configuration (a specific instance of the underdeveloped-developed connection), and the colored-white relationship. Although these overlap, each gives rise to different emphases in explanation and stresses different aspects of the ongoing interaction. It is obvious that to select only one characterization distorts the genesis and the assessment of the patterns of relationships developing in Britain.

IMMIGRANT STATUS AND
CULTURAL DIVERSITY

The position of colored people in Britain is frequently attributed to their status as relatively newly arrived migrants. The new migrant is isolated from the dominant group by cultural factors that make him distinctive and noticeable. The colored migrant is considered the "archetypal stranger." The experience of Irish and Jewish immigrants to Britain is cited as evidence that strangeness is the cause of the problem and not color. As the second and subsequent generations, growing up in a new environment, discard their strange distinguishing characteristics, the separateness and hostility will disappear. The earlier immigrants are assumed to have followed a pattern of adjustment leading to social uniformity within an integrated British structure. Particularly in the case of poor immigrants, there are many similarities in the initial situation: for the migrants, they include finding work and accommodation, as well as coping with the multiplicity of conflicting experiences in an alien environment; for the indigenous population, they include meeting with people whose different customs, habits, and language are not always understood or accepted, and who are in competition with them for jobs, homes, and social services. There is a remarkable similarity, too, in the arguments and phrases in which opposition to immigrants is expressed. Allegations that "it is only a matter of time before the population becomes entirely foreign . . . . The rates are burdened with the education of thousands of children of foreign parents . . ."[2] as well as threats of violent reactions from the indigenous population whose jobs, homes, and entire way of life are seen to be jeopardized are as familiar in the 1960s as they were in the 1900s.

Despite the similarities, two aspects of the problem are ignored. First, the strict parallels between white and colored migrants neglect the social relevance attached to color—a characteristic that cannot be discarded. Insofar as color is a socially distinguishing characteristic, not only the newly arrived but also their descendants are distinctive. There is little evidence to support the contention that the indigenous colored are treated any the less as colored than the newly arrived. The children of colored migrants who have grown up in Britain do not experience less difficulty in getting work, for instance, than their parents. The evidence points to the redefining of British-born colored people as immigrants as a rationalization of differential treatment that seeks to avoid the stigma of color discrimination.

With respect to the second aspect, it cannot be assumed that the discarding of external characteristics such as language, accent, foreign dress, and habits among those of Irish or Jewish descent implies a pattern of social uniformity. Adherence to a minority religion persists as a potential and, in some cases, an actual source of structural differentiation. Religious intolerance is less marked in British society now than in times when it was claimed that "we very much doubt whether in England, or indeed in any free Protestant country, a true Papist can be a good subject."[3] For instance, in British areas with heavy Irish settlement and, more particularly, in Northern Ireland, religious differentiation is an integral part of the structure; it affects employment, housing, and educational prospects and is reflected in political allegiance. Elsewhere many overt forms of religious differentiation have disappeared. Where, however, minority religions are coupled with factors such as preferred intermarriage, local residence patterns, separate educational provision, or differential socialization, identity as a group remains.

In the case of Indians, West Indians, and Pakistanis both the persistence of some degree of group identity based on primary socialization within minority groups and the creation of such an identity through differential treatment by the white population are becoming evident in Britain. Culturally their position is comparable to that of the Jews and Irish insofar as they adhere to minority religions. The Sikhs, Muslims, and Hindus are cases in point. They are concerned with transmitting religious beliefs and practices, establishing associations to provide facilities for this transmission on a community basis, and obtaining concessions for the practice of their religion. Cultural differences are not regarded as neutral variations in customs and habits. Socially, they are hierarchically organized in terms of prestige and often in terms of power. For instance, those who diverge from the dominant cultural habits have to justify their differences and extract concessions in order to observe religious practices or particular modes of dress or marriage customs. Among the Muslim and Sikh communities, the process of extracting such concessions has been one of the foremost pressures in forming organizations. In some spheres this brings them into direct conflict with other groups in the society, and, in particular, problems have arisen in employment and education. The resolution of this kind of problem can be seen as part of a process of accommodation. Some degree of secularization and anglicization on the part of the minorities, in addition to acceptance of defined and limited deviations by the dominant groups, is already taking place. The persistence of culturally diverse factors is potentially divisive in social interaction. Separation of spheres of activity serves to minimize such conflictual interaction. In an industrial society where employment and, to a large extent, formal education involve interaction between those of diverse cultural backgrounds, such separation of activity is possible only to a very limited degree.

The minorities are exposed to the customs, habits, and beliefs of the dominant group, particularly in education and in the patterns of occupational opportunity. While they must learn something of the ways of the dominant group, it is usual for them to continue to be exposed to the minority culture that they are expected to regard as their own. Socialization within a minority family is likely to be intensely oriented toward highly valued aspects of that culture, and where it has been the experience of the group to meet discrimination, however remote in time, rejection of these aspects involves highly charged sentiments. On the psychological level, it involves rejection of elements of personal identity. Psychological security may rest on ties that set them apart from the larger community. Positive and negative aspects of group identity are transmitted and expressed in a variety of ways, often seemingly trivial, but meaningful to those who share the common identity. The communal identity is part of the inheritance of many descendants of earlier immigrants who are not distinguished by external characteristics nor strict adherents of minority religions. There is no reason to assume that such group identity will not persist among many of the children of Indians, West Indians, and Pakistanis. Their interaction within the wider society and processes of secondary socialization present alternative evaluations and conflicting ways of behaving. This, however, does not necessarily lead to psychological or social maladjustment of the "cultural hybrids" stressed by Stonequist in his discussion of marginal men.[4] It has been argued that ". . . if an alternative world appears in secondary socialisation, the individual may opt for it in a manipulative manner . . . . The individual internalises the new reality, but instead of it being *his* reality, it is used by him for specific purposes."[5] This approach gives a fuller understanding of persistence of minority identity even with participation in the dominant structure than the approaches that emphasize psychological or social maladjustment or assume that a process of assimilation or integration is characteristic of second and subsequent generations. The pressures toward some forms of integration with the wider society and the preservation of a separate identity are common problematic experiences of minority groups.[6] This internal division and the positions adopted are not matters settled merely by the groups themselves. Where differential and particularly disadvantageous treatment accrues from minority identity, the problem becomes more acute. The minority identity is reinforced and therefore more easily maintained, but the pressures toward individual assimilation are increased while the chances of group integration are decreased. The individual and group choices between alternatives are circumscribed by the structure of the wider society.

THE COLONIAL HERITAGE

The treatment of colored groups in Britain and their response patterns cannot be separated from the overall context of present and former relationships within the British Commonwealth. Although the early stages of empire building may be summed up as "gold, glory, and gospel," the development in complexity and scope of British imperialism and the subsequent transformation into the Commonwealth defy such brief description. The political and economic forces behind the development were numerous and interacting, and the view that the Empire was acquired "in a fit of absence of mind" distorts the pressures within Europe toward imperial expansion. Equally the perspective that asserts that the explanation lies in "the last stages of monopoly capitalism" simplifies not only the causes but the consequences of this expansion and its later developments.[7] These various approaches and many more are part, however, of the inherited belief system of members of the Commonwealth and, as such, affect the relations between the white and colored who now find themselves involved in direct social interaction within Britain itself.

First, the asymmetrical relationship of Britain as the dominant society within an association populated largely by colored peoples to each of Britain's former possessions and second, the relationship between the wide variety of societies and peoples within the association itself are of particular relevance. These gave rise to differential politico-economic structures and experiences that produced not a common identity but positions of relative superordination-subordination and wide discrepancies in attitudes and expectations in relation to one another.

The more directly apparent relationship is between Britain and each of her former colonies. Attitudes toward colored people were in practice largely irrelevant in Britain itself before the 1950s. There were few situations in which whites were called upon to interact directly with colored people and almost none in which they had to decide domestic policies in relation to the colored people in Britain. However, this apparent irrelevance cannot be taken to mean that such attitudes did not exist. Britain's position as the dominant society in an Empire with large colored populations had affected the structure and the fabric of British society in innumerable ways. Particular stereotypes of colored colonial subjects that did not emphasize their Britishness but their dependence, backwardness, and lack of "character," had been fostered by the school, church, and army. Some stereotypes of inferiority had been built up and reinforced over long periods of time and had become an integral part of

168 · New Minorities, Old Conflicts

British attitudes. In 1792, for instance, the Governor General of Bengal declared that he believed every native of Hindostan to be corrupt; in 1897 Lord Roberts claimed that evidence could be bought on any subject and that however brave, well-educated, and adept a native might be he would not be considered as an equal by the British officer; in 1921 an official committee on Indianization of the army thought it would take forty years and that segregation might be a possible solution to the difficulty of getting white officers to serve under Indian officers.[8] Even though "nineteen people out of twenty, the middle class and most of the lower class knew no more of the Empire than they did of the Argentine Republic or of the Italian Renaissance,"[9] this did not prevent acceptance of the idea that to be colored was to be different and therefore, on the whole, inferior. Tolerance and patronage frequently marked attitudes toward the subject peoples in far-away colored possessions. The exact nature of the supposed inferiority need not be spelled out in any detail as the firmly established systems of ethnic inequality prevented economic and social competition. As Commonwealth people arrived in Britain to work and live alongside the local population the contradictions in the attitudes of tolerance and the expectations of dominance-submission became sharper. The resulting antagonism came to be expressed gradually and unevenly in color conflicts.

This was particularly so in the many instances where a differential understanding and emphasis was placed on the relationship by immigrants. For example, the common feeling among many West Indians that they were British with a right to live and work in Britain and an expectation that they would be treated as such was derived from socialization in the West Indies that promoted such feelings toward Britain as the "mother country." This differed markedly from the general attitude in Britain where the question of such inalienable rights of entry became a highly controversial matter and where "Britishness" and color were not a readily accepted combination.

Further the relations of economic and political interdependence are differentially evaluated by the various groups, leading to misunderstanding and hostility in the present situation. It is not possible to gauge accurately how many Indians still share the view expressed by Pandit Nehru that ". . . nearly all our major problems today have grown up during British rule and as a direct result of British policy, . . . the minority problem; various vested interests, foreign and Indian; the lack of industry and the neglect of agriculture; the extreme backwardness in the social services; and, above all, the tragic poverty of the people."[10] Nor is it necessary to accept that this view is a valid statement of Britain's relationship with India, but to disregard the part it plays in determining attitudes and behavior is to ignore one important aspect of the present situation in which migrants from the Commonwealth interact with whites. Britain's imperial role and its current consequences are evaluated very differently by many whites who are socialized to view it primarily as a humane, civilizing, and beneficial, if frequently hazardous, endeavor. The expectations of each group are based on experience, ideas, and interests developed under very different conditions, and a lack of congruence is evident in the interpretations of many situations. Many forms of behavior accepted as reasonable or normal by white groups are seen, or anticipated, by colored groups to be a continuation of an unequal relationship. For example, the special knowledge and skills of those with colonial experience is thought by white groups to equip them to carry out integration work with immigrants as liaison or welfare officers. Colored immigrant groups see this as an extension of the colonial superordinate-subordinate relationship into the British context. The consequences of such contradictory interpretations are very far-reaching in their effects on the relations developing between colored and white in Britain.

The ties of Empire and Commonwealth were largely centered on the relationship of Britain toward the other societies; but this had consequences for the relationships of the dependent societies themselves. One such consequence was the movement of people from Asia, particularly India, to parts of British-held Africa and to the West Indies. The political and economic ties were not sufficient to produce a communal identity between, for instance, the West Indian territories or India and Pakistan. Colored migrants from the Commonwealth did not arrive in Britain with a sense of shared identity with each other. The divisions as we saw in Chapter 3 were, and still are, very marked in many cases. These are due in part to wide cultural and geographical separation and in part to the differential treatment and position within the colonial context. Feelings of difference and antagonism between, for instance, Indians from India and those coming from East Africa or between those of African or Indian descent from the West Indies cannot be understood without reference to Britain's role in creating their differential political and economic experience.[11] The developing of a common identity among colored migrants from the Commonwealth owes little to the past and is to be explained much more in terms of their present experience in Britain, including attempts to forge such an identity based on an ideology of past common exploitation.

THE DEVELOPMENT OF COLOR CONSCIOUSNESS

The expression of color consciousness has generally increased in Britain among whites and non-whites during the past decade. The explanation of this development, however, its strength and distribution among the population, and its relation to action presents a number of difficult problems. The difficulties arise not only from the absence of much relevant empirical data but from the lack of an adequate sociological model for analyzing the many variables and mechanisms that are part of such a process. A full explanation of the process would involve a consideration of the interrelationships of the psychological, social, economic, and political determinants within the context of the development of British society, a task well beyond the scope of this book. At this point, we can outline briefly only the particular forms of color consciousness developing in Britain. We have seen some of the influences of the immigrant status and of the socio-historical context that are present in the situation and underlie the direct interaction of white and colored. It is within these that the impact of immediate experiences must be assessed.

We are not dealing with a systematic ideology or belief system about color or racial differences. The existence of a coherent, potent, explicit racialist ideology, for instance, is not part of the belief system of white or colored groups in Britain as it is, for example, among the whites in South Africa. This does not mean that there are no individuals who subscribe to such an ideology or that small groups do not expound such beliefs; however, as yet, this has not become an integral, coherent, and accepted way of thought. We are dealing with a "common sense view of the world." This commonsense view is incoherent and contradictory but has a generalized meaning in everyday thought and, as such, can be communicated and serve as a basis for action.[12] It is within this form of consciousness that color has become a meaningful category, inconsistently linked with other categories of racial tolerance and notions of social justice.

The processes by which groups are identified in terms of color or any other supposed or actual ethnic differences are part of a more general process of social differentiation. It is one of the many possible ways of categorizing social groups. Categories, whether of objects, events, or people, facilitate the processes of social interaction. Apart from our closest associates, we place others into categories and treat them as though they were alike. Where complete strangers are concerned, we work on superficial cues of dress, facial expression, vocabulary, and accent, for instance. Many of our dealings are neither with very close associates nor with complete strangers but with others in well-defined social situations. From the situation we know how to behave toward the others involved. Our systems of categorization do not depend only on immediate situations or on direct contact but are developed on the basis of commonsense knowledge transmitted by a variety of means such as mass communication, gossip, folk beliefs, and parental and peer group influences. We learn by participating in organized social activity, which conditions our actions but, in turn, can be transformed by our reactions and redefinitions. The utility of this process for social interaction is obvious; but it also involves the possibility of the categories becoming objectified in such a way that many forms of interaction are prescribed for us. Particular ways of behaving are accepted at the expense of other courses of action. Patterns of interaction are facilitated and inhibited by the same process. For example, when our direct experience is contrary to the conventionally accepted categorization, we may be unable to change our ways of thinking and acting. Or we may retain our original categorization but modify our behavior by making exceptions in particular instances. This is seen in the case commonly encountered in interracial personal contact: a particular individual is redefined as "friend," "cricketer," or "professor" but the categories, Jew or West Indian, for instance, are retained as generalized conceptions for all other members of the group.

Although it may be the case that "human beings interact not so much in terms of what they actually are but in terms of the conceptions that they form of themselves and of one another,"[13] the processes of commonsense consciousness and the mechanisms of categorization within them are part of sociohistorical structures, varying in content and form, at different times, in different societies.

After almost two decades of colored immigration, color has become increasingly a distinguishing characteristic. Physical differences of color have become translated into social differences. Behavior has developed that imputes social meaning to this particular physical difference, and relations between colored and white are commonly defined as problematic. This development of color awareness is commonly attributed to recent changes in the composition of the population, namely, the arrival of people from Asia and the Caribbean and is also attributed to direct social interaction between the whites and the colored. It is often maintained that this is a "natural" reaction among those who believe others to be physically different from themselves, and attitudes of antagonism and discriminatory relations are inevitable social processes. This mechanistic explanation ignores the weight of evidence that people react differently and impute different meanings to physical characteristics according to the total situation in which they find themselves. The degree to which color awareness has developed and the ways in which it manifests itself in behavior are questions for the social scientists to analyze and explain. For instance, although some relations between white and colored are marked by the characteristics of antagonism and some patterns of discrimination have developed, equally cooperative relations and an ignoring of this particular physical difference are evident in other areas of social life. While the chances of seeing colored people and the likelihood of working with or living near them have increased, the vast majority of the population experiences no such direct social contact and the expression of color consciousness has not been shown to be greater or more widespread among those who do. Two elements that have been of particular relevance to the increase in color awareness are the general politicization of race and the emphasis on the association of color and social problems, both of which were discussed in Chapter 2. These have affected the responses of both colored and white in the definition of the problem, its causes and consequences, and the choice of solutions now open.

MULTIRACIALISM, INTEGRATION OR SEPARATISM?

The race situation in Britain is still essentially one of transition. There are no long established traditions of how colored and white treat each other in formal or informal situations as there are, for instance, in the Southern states of America or as there were in the British colonial situation. Nor is the position of colored groups in relation to white fixed in a system of ethnic stratification. The relationships are frequently marked by ambivalent attitudes and conflicting expectations of which many of the actors are only half-aware. This is so in spite of the events and pressures of the past decade toward a clearer drawing of color distinctions. The problems and prospects of developing a positive multiracial society are reflected in the various attempts to form voluntary organizations and the interaction of these with the official approach to the race situation.

There is in Britain no organization comparable to the civil rights movement in the United States. Over the past ten years, concern has been expressed that something be done to prevent the development of discrimination, hostility, and violence between the white and colored groups. This concern has produced, on the negative side, policies of restricting immigration, as well as suggestions of repatriation, curtailed residence, and enforced dispersals, but it has also led to agitation to outlaw racial discrimination and to a variety of organizations aimed at promoting tolerance and understanding. The composition of these organizations and the activities in which they engage vary, depending on how they define the problems to be overcome and the methods they adopt to pursue their aims.

It is useful to classify the groups into three types differentiated by the overall aims and the definition of the problem. These types refer to predominant emphases, but in many groups, particularly in the early stages, combinations of all three approaches coexisted. The first approach aimed at integration with the stress on the immigrants changing and fitting in with British society and the question of color was largely ignored. The problem was seen as stemming from the presence of immigrants unaccustomed to the British way of life and as a result provoking hostility and exacerbating problems by such behavior as overcrowding in congested urban areas. The second was concerned with establishing the idea of cultural pluralism, encouraging each immigrant group to retain some of its own customs but conforming in other ways to prevent conflicts with the host society. In this case the problem was seen largely in terms of cultural differences that produced antagonism if left unexplained. In the third, the emphasis was on pursuing full political and economic equality of colored with white and the problems were considered to be related to the color divisions that coincided with differential power positions. The activities of the groups differed in accordance with the degree of emphasis given to one or another of these approaches.

Early Voluntary Groups

Until 1964 the efforts remained largely on a voluntary basis; voluntary groups were chronically short of funds and manpower and frequently uncertain of the problems or how to tackle them. Many groups had a short life, more had largely inactive or ineffective roles in their local community. They were often supported by prominent locals, such as mayors, ministers of religion, councillors, and members of Parliament. Some promoted social activities through which "immigrants" and "hosts" could meet. Agreeable social occasions in themselves, they tended to be elite gatherings at which the facts of discrimination, violence, or simply the difficulties encountered in coping with an urban industrial life were not raised or discussed. Their function was limited to introducing the most articulate, educated immigrants to tolerant whites. Other groups carried out advisory, welfare, and education activities that dealt with problems of individuals or attempted through public meetings, discussion groups, and leaflets to inform the public of the background of the immigrants living in their locality; they ran English classes or classes on the English way of life for the immigrants themselves. In addition, such activities were sometimes combined with conciliation functions to settle misunderstandings and hostilities that arose, particularly between white and colored neighbors. Some branched out further, sponsoring multiracial youth clubs, housing associations, and tackling the intricacies of local bureaucracies in an attempt to solve housing or education problems. Teachers, doctors, clergy, trade unionists, housewives, employers, students, and apprentices came forward in many areas to initiate and support the work. The groups remained predominantly white and predominantly middle class and, in this sense, unrepresentative either of the immigrant or the white population. There were some notable exceptions that had much closer links with the colored groups and with representatives of local labor movements. The Southall International Friendship Committee received financial support from trade unions. The Willesden International Friendship Committee, as well as running successful social activities, tackled such problems as relations with the local police and actively considered the policy of the local educational authority.

The differences in aims and methods remained latent in some groups, but the changing atmosphere of the 1960s brought the conflicting approaches into sharp focus in others. This led to fragmentation and differentiation. For some, the growing evidence of discrimination in housing, education, and employment, the politicizing of race at local and national levels, and the categorization and differentiation implicit in immigration control demonstrated the necessity of explicit and organized multiracial opposition to racialism. The groups stressed the necessity of active involvement of colored people in organization and attributed an equal role in the devising and initiating of practical activities at all levels to colored and white. Others continued to see the question as one of removing the problems created by the arrival of immigrants and seeking ways of integrating them into the British way of life, and thus the dominant role was to be played by the white members advised and assisted by leaders drawn from the immigrant communities. It is not possible to determine how this basic conflict of aims and methods would have been resolved between the groups had they continued to develop without the intervention of the government.

Official Action and the Work of Liaison Committees

The Home Secretary had appointed an advisory council in 1962 to advise him on matters he decided were affecting the welfare of Commonwealth immigrants and their integration. On the council's recommendation, a National Council for Commonwealth Immigrants was set up on April 1, 1964, and a fulltime advisory officer was appointed to coordinate and encourage local effort. In the autumn of 1965, following the White Paper on Commonwealth Immigration, the National Committee was re-formed and a local and regional committee structure was outlined.[14] The committee system remained voluntary but with paid full-time officials serving on local and national levels. The National Committee and the local committees were not under direct government control. Close liaison was expected, however, and official financial assistance could be used as a sanction. The committees had no sanctions over activities of government departments either local or national and these could, and did on occasion, conflict directly with the work of "positively promoting goodwill."[15] When the government failed to take notice of the National Committee over the question of Kenyan-Asian immigration, for instance, the committee could only threaten to resign.* At the local level, policies inimical to

---

* This threat was withdrawn after the passing of the act, with the exception of two members of the staff and a few panel members.

the promotion of confidence and goodwill in housing, education, and health were either not questioned by the committees
or, where questioned, little was achieved. No officials were required to meet and consult committee members and, apart
from publicity, there was little that could be done by the national or local committees to bring pressure to bear. It was
assumed that any conflicts of policy would be resolved by close
liaison carried out at the local level by liaison officers.

Liaison officers of local committees were placed in a structurally ambiguous situation. They were to serve the local committees, be advised, and, in some cases, trained by the National
Committee; they were to build up the trust and confidence of
immigrant groups and maintain close liaison and cooperation
with officials of the local authority. Their selection, appointment, and financial backing reflected these varying and often
conflicting interests. The question of the ethnic background of
liaison officers was of crucial importance in many areas in
gaining confidence of local immigrant groups. Previous local
experience and loyalties raised delicate issues, in some cases,
about their attitude toward immigrants. Those responsible for
appointments seemed unaware or defeated by the complexities
of these situations. In addition, the structure of conflicting interests within which liaison officers worked handicapped many
of them in formulating and carrying out positive policies, and
the way in which some came to define their jobs and the methods they employed further incapacitated them in carrying out
at least some of the tasks they were called upon to perform.
Individual officers solved the problem for themselves by identi-
fying either with local authority policies, or with particular
groups of immigrants, or with particular sections of their committees. Many retreated into peripheral, noncontroversial activities. The failure of many liaison officers to play an active
part in improving the climate of race relations stems not from
individual failings or personality differences but from the conflicts inherent in the structure in which they are employed and
the dilemma about the aims of their work, which the official
definition of "integration into the community" did little to
resolve.[16]

The steps advocated by the government in its 1965 white

paper and many statements since, while insisting that there can be no question of allowing Commonwealth immigrants to be regarded as second-class citizens, direct attention to problems that their presence creates for, among others, local authorities. These problems center particularly around housing, education, and health. For instance, "the main cause of unsatisfactory living conditions among immigrants is the multiple occupation of houses originally designed for one family." "About one-third of immigrant children is the maximum that is normally acceptable in a school if social strains are to be avoided and educational standards maintained." And concerning health, ". . . many immigrants will for a variety of reasons continue to impose a relatively heavy burden on the health services . . . . Their needs are different in degree rather than in kind."[17] The consequences of such official statements have been to legitimate the association of color and problems and to emphasize the immigrant problem as a focus of the work for integration rather than to deal with the broader question of race relations. Although the National Committee in jointly sponsoring investigations into discrimination in employment and into the question of extending legislation against discrimination did not totally confine itself to "immigrant problems" and neglect the wider issues of race relations, the regional and local levels have taken a much narrower view.

This narrow perspective was further encouraged by the separation of the work of the local liaison committees from that of the local conciliation committees set up under the Race Relations Board to investigate complaints of racial discrimination.* The board itself, consisting of three part-time members appointed for one year, had no express powers to investigate complaints and no powers to undertake conciliation. Five area com-

---

* The Race Relations Act of 1965 was the first legislation in Britain to establish the illegality of discrimination on grounds of race, color, ethnic, or national origin. It applied to public places and covered only certain kinds of discrimination. It did not cover employment or housing nor did it apply to "The Crown," which includes all government departments and premises. Sections concerned with incitement to racial hatred and breaches of public order were included in the act, but the Race Relations Board had no power to deal with these sections.[18]

mittees appointed by the board worked on a voluntary basis with the help of full-time conciliation officers of whom there were three at the beginning of 1967. These committees covered large areas and many of the difficulties they faced arose from the deficiencies in the act itself, which was extremely narrowly framed and unclear on a number of points.

The structure into which much of the work of voluntary liaison committees was organized was directed by the government's approach to integration, and the separation of the problems of discrimination from the work of the voluntary committees increased the difficulties of those concerned with a broader view of the problem. There was a tendency for the work to be carried on remote from the immigrant communities and their problems; there was little encouragement to develop tolerance and understanding of the race question for either white or colored people. And most complaints of discrimination fell outside the act, but, above all, an atmosphere of cynicism and despair became evident in colored communities where they not only endured the problems but were increasingly assumed to *cause* them. The tasks of setting up local and national committees representative of the people who experience the housing, education, and employment problems, and evolving policies to deal with these problems, and developing racial tolerance could not be tackled within the framework established by the government.*

Unofficial Groups after 1964

Groups independent of the semiofficial structure of the liaison and conciliation committees developed in some areas. They were critical of prevailing policies and more concerned with equal rights and removing abuses than with "immigrant prob-

---

* In October 1968 the Community Relations Commission replaced the National Committee for Commonwealth Immigrants, but many of the conflicts inherent in the earlier structure were inherited and its activities continued along broadly similar lines. About half the commission's budget was allocated to building up local activities. Eighty Community Relations Councils with fifty-three full-time officers existed throughout the country, but there was little change in the scope and type of activity. Finance for an urban area program was administered by the Home Office in conjunction with local authority efforts.

lems." A few such local organizations that had existed before the officially recognized bodies did not amalgamate with them. The Campaign for Racial Equality in Leicester and the Coordinating Committee against Racial Discrimination in Birmingham are instances of such local bodies. They continued to provide information and carry out conciliation functions, social activities, and help individual cases, doing work similar to that carried out by the semiofficial liaison committees, but they also collected information on discrimination by public or private bodies and attempted to redress them through "respectable" channels, using political pressure and demonstration when necessary. They encouraged immigrants to join trade unions, political parties, and to register as voters. Their continued existence, unlike that of the semiofficial bodies, depended partly on results and on a continuing recognition of the possibility of a different structure of race relations. They succeeded in gaining broader immigrant support and involvement, but their activities were handicapped by lack of resources and they have not achieved a grass roots organization nor coordinated their work on a national basis.

Most of these existing groups affiliated with the Campaign Against Racial Discrimination (C.A.R.D.), established in 1965 to expose discrimination as well as demand political action and legislation. New groups sprang up in many localities. The promise of a nationally coordinated movement was not realized, however, and in December 1967, the serious differences already existing nationally within C.A.R.D. came to the surface. The repercussions of these differences affected the local groups less adversely than the work of coordinating policies and activities on a national level.

On the issues of antidiscriminatory legislation and immigration policy some measure of national coordination has been achieved. An Equal Rights Campaign, organized largely by former supporters of C.A.R.D., acted for some months during 1968 for the limited objective of securing improvements and extensions in the race relations bill. They disbanded when the bill was passed. The Joint Council for Welfare of Immigrants (J.C.W.I.) was initiated jointly by the Indian Workers' Association (Southall), C.A.R.D., and the West Indian Standing Conference in September 1967 to deal with immigration matters. It succeeded in getting the support of a large number of organizations, both immigrant and multiracial, and over half the voluntary liaison committees and the National Committee for Commonwealth Immigrants became associated with it. The relative success of the J.C.W.I. in getting broad-based support has been attributed to several reasons: the fact that initiative came from immigrant organizations, the relatively restricted field of the council's operations, and the unifying nature of the problem of immigration, a factor that concerns all immigrant and alien communities. As well as organizing opposition to the Immigration Act of 1968, the council was able to secure representation in Home Office discussions on the Wilson Committee Report on Immigration Appeals,* but, most importantly, it was able to act independently and employ a full-time worker to aid individuals experiencing immigration problems.

The Contemporary Situation

All multiracial organizations have been weakened by the increasing discriminatory effects of national and local policies. Their apparent inability to act effectively has reduced the confidence of both colored and white members. The semiofficial bodies never had strong links with colored organizations; at the national level the Indian Workers' Association (Great Britain) had consistently refused to collaborate, and the West Indian Standing Conference and the National Federation of Pakistani Associations were divided on the issue from the beginning and,

---

* The difficulties of administering the legislation relating to control of entry and deportation of Commonwealth citizens and the resulting public criticisms by organizations and individuals led to the setting up of a committee in 1966 "to consider whether any, and, if so what, rights of appeal or other remedies should be available to aliens and Commonwealth citizens who are refused admission to, or required to leave the country." The Wilson Committee, named after its chairman, Sir Roy Wilson, Queen's Council, reported in August 1967. Its terms of reference excluded any recommendations for changes in controlling immigration. The report makes a number of recommendations for changes in the rights of aliens and Commonwealth citizens, particularly in the instituting of an appeals system for those refused entry and extending and enlarging appeals against deportation orders.[19]

after an initial liaison, left or became alienated from the work of the National Committee for Commonwealth Immigrants. C.A.R.D., setting out at the national level, later encouraged the formation of local groups. The most important immigrant organizations either did not affiliate or withdrew active cooperation, and liaison committees, with few exceptions, did not affiliate. At the local level there were instances of cooperation between the liaison committees, immigrant organizations, and the unofficial "campaign" committees. Much depended on the ability of local members to overcome the handicaps of divergent approaches. The basic incompatibilities between the aims, policies, and methods of the organizations meant that even this level of cooperation had virtually disappeared by the end of 1967. Liaison committees were seen increasingly as an instrument of both local and national government, providing a blanket by which discriminatory practices could be followed under the guise of seeking integration. There are many examples of local colored representatives who, wishing to follow a positive policy of uncovering and remedying local abuses, were actively discouraged, discredited as unrepresentative or troublemakers, or simply excluded by technicalities from playing any part in local policymaking. Their aims upset the influential and the respectable. The experience of the 1965 white paper and the 1968 Immigration Act combined to destroy many immigrant groups' confidence in the liaison committee's structure and methods having any relevance to the solution of race problems.

The failure of local campaign committees to establish an anti-racialist movement on a national basis or even to develop strong roots in a local movement was due to a number of factors. The practical difficulties of a few people without resources of money, time, or power to tackle the various manifestations of a deteriorating race-relations situation led to attempts at spreading the resources too broadly and to constant self-questioning of the effectiveness of the committee's efforts. They were unable to demonstrate, except in minor instances, their ability to meet the problems developing in local communities and, as such, were unable to justify their policy or methods to the majority of colored people within their areas. An awareness of the need for the active participation of the mass of local colored groups did not, in itself, produce either the means or the conditions for such participation. As the situation worsened, it appeared that although local liaison committees were effective in pursuing their policies, the members of campaign committees were ineffective in countering them. The capacity and the intentions of such groups were inevitably suspect in such a situation.

It was within this situation that the idea of a movement organized largely by and for colored people to oppose racialism began to grow. Previously the advocates of such a movement had been seen as extremists copying the American movement. Many colored and white opponents of racialism who sympathized with the frustration and anger were convinced of the irrelevance and powerlessness of such a movement in British conditions. The questions that arise in connection with the establishing of such an organization, unified on the basis of color in the British context, are of two kinds: What conditions exist to make such a movement possible, and how effective could such a movement be? The failure to distinguish between these two questions has led to a great deal of confusion both among the proponents and opponents of such a movement.

The development of such organizations within British society is problematic. The common experience of differential treatment on grounds of color, the failure of an effective white opposition to racialism, and the weakness of multiracial organizations constitute strong social pressures toward color consciousness and the acceptance of the belief that color is the only effective basis of organization. Neither potential leaders of a movement based on color nor the majority of colored immigrants are necessarily aware of the fact that many white people also experience bad housing, poor educational provision, and restriction of employment opportunities. Insofar as they associate color discrimination with the cause of their problems, support for separatist organizations appears relevant. On the other hand, the internal divisions of the colored population stemming from socioeconomic differences in Britain and from the wide variations in backgrounds pose problems for unity of purpose and direction. Attempts at unity, such as the Black People's Alliance, have arisen as a response to public manifestations of racialism. To be successful such groups will have to develop a consciousness of the common life chances of the majority of colored immigrants and, more especially, the chances of colored children. In addition, there must be a realization of the relevance of organizing as colored groups to improve their position and protest at the injustices of inequality. Many immigrant organizations themselves are now divided on this issue of building a separate colored movement or one that incorporates white supporters.

This division relates partly to the question of how effective a separate movement could be vis-á-vis the dominant white structure. The colored population is extremely small. In no area or occupation do they form concentrations of political or economic power. The lack of objective sources of power cannot be overcome simply through a heightened consciousness of the disadvantages attached to colored groups and of the necessity for action to remedy this. It is the recognition of this that partially explains the continued attempts to build a more effective multiracial movement.[20]

How far such attempts can be successful remains debatable. It depends not only on the ability of white and colored people to recruit wider support and evolve policies and methods more appropriate to the problems but also on much broader social developments. In particular, any multiracial movement must work within the context of the activities of the various power groups in the dominant structure. For whatever specific reason, as long as these power groups adopt practices that continue to attribute social meaning to color differences, the possibility of a multiracial movement will be weakened. The choice will be more clearly between either the acceptance of second-class citizenship through patterns of submission or avoidance or rejection of inferior citizenship through separate organizations marked by withdrawal or aggression.

Notes

[1] For a fuller discussion of some of the theoretical and methodological problems involved, see Max Weber, *General Economic History* (New York: Collier, 1961); Max Weber, *The Methodology of the Social Sciences,* ed. and trans. by Edward A. Shils

and Henry A. Finch (New York: Free Press, 1949); P. S. Cohen, "Models," *British Journal of Sociology*, 17 (March 1966), 70–78.

2 Member of Parliament for Stepney, speech on immigration control (London: January 29, 1902) in Paul Foot, *Immigration and Race in British Politics* (Baltimore: Penguin, 1965), pp. 88–89.

3 The *Times*, March 3, 1853, in John Archer Jackson, *The Irish in Britain* (London: Routledge and Kegan Paul, 1963), p. 155.

4 Everett V. Stonequist, *The Marginal Man* (New York: Russell and Russell, 1960), Chapter III.

5 Peter L. Berger and Thomas Luckmann, *The Social Construction of Reality* (London: Allen Lane, 1967), p. 192.

6 For a discussion of comparative evidence on this point, see Tamotsu Shibutani and Kian M. Kwan, *Ethnic Stratification: A Comparative Approach* (New York: © Copyright, THE MAC-MILLAN COMPANY, 1965), pp. 502–515.

7 Assessments by historians, economists, and political scientists reach varying conclusions about the causes and consequences of the relationship between Britain and her overseas territories. For a historical review of some of the dominant ideas and their contemporary relevance, see A. P. Thornton, *Doctrines of Imperialism* (New York: Wiley, 1965); Eric Stokes, *The Political Ideas of English Imperialism* (London: Oxford University Press, 1960); for an assessment of economic relationships, see Richard Koebner, "The Concept of Economic Imperialism," *Economic History Review*, Vol. 2, series ii, no. 1 (April 1949); S. B. Saul, *Studies in British Overseas Trade 1870–1914* (Liverpool: Liverpool University Press, 1960), Chapter VIII. This latter work deals with trade with India.
The "classic" works on the subject of imperialism are J. A. Hobson, *Imperialism*, 3rd. ed. (London: G. Allen and Unwin, 1938); V. I. Lenin, *Imperialism, The Highest Stage of Capitalism* (Moscow: Foreign Languages Publishing House, n.d.); Joseph Schumpeter, *Imperialism and Social Classes*, Bert Hoselitz, ed. (New York: Meridian Books, 1955).

8 Thornton, *op. cit.*, p. 171.

9 H. G. Wells, *Mr. Britling Sees it Through* (London: Cassell and Co., 1916) in Thornton, *op. cit.*, p. 90.

10 J. Nehru, *The Discovery of India* (London: Asia Publishing House, 1961), p. 323.

11 See M. Klass, *East Indians in Trinidad: A Study of Cultural Persistence* (New York: Columbia University Press, 1961);

Thornton, *op. cit.*, p. 175. The policy of "divide and rule" was marked by differing degrees of effectiveness and whether it was intentional is an open question and need not concern us; there is no doubt that it is one factor, among others, in creating and perpetuating religious, cultural, and "racial" differences and conflict.

12 For a critical explanation of the emergence and transformation of such views in relation to social groups, see Antonio Gramsci, *The Modern Prince and Other Writings*, L. Marks, trans. (London: Lawrence and Wishart, 1967), pp. 90–117; for a discussion of the social psychological mechanisms involved, see Berger and Luckmann, *op. cit.*, Part 2.

13 Shibutani and Kwan, *op. cit.*, p. 38. Reproduced by permission.

14 The Commonwealth Immigrants Advisory Council was a voluntary committee that produced three reports on housing, education, and employment. They were Command Papers 2119, 2266, and 2458 respectively. In 1964 the National Committee for Commonwealth Immigrants was appointed to give advice and information and encourage the establishing of local and regional voluntary liaison committees. It held a meeting of representatives of existing committees on April 1, 1965. The white paper (*Immigration from the Commonwealth*, Cmnd. 2739 [London: H.M.S.O., August 1965], Part III) dealt with integration. It set out certain problem areas—housing, education, employment, and health, referred to the possibility of financial assistance to local areas where special need was shown, and outlined the structure and functions of the National Committee and its association with regional and local voluntary liaison committees. Three "conditions for success" of local liaison committees were laid down, covering composition, relationship to local authorities, and a nonsectarian, nonpolitical basis. It was proposed that a full-time, salaried, trained official should serve each committee, and financial assistance toward the cost of employing a suitably qualified person was offered. The National Committee for Commonwealth Immigrants was appointed by the Prime Minister in September 1965 under the chairmanship of the Archbishop of Canterbury to promote and coordinate on a national basis efforts directed toward the integration of Commonwealth immigrants into the community.

15 *Immigration from the Commonwealth, op. cit.*, p. 17.

16 An unusually perceptive account of some of the problems can be found in John Kassie, "First Impressions as a Liaison Officer," *Liaison*, no. 7 (London: National Committee for Commonwealth Immigrants, April 1967), pp. 7–9.

17 *Immigration from the Commonwealth, op. cit.,* pp. 11–14.

18 The board issued its first report in April 1967 which reviewed the structure of conciliation work and the problems arising. See "Report of the Race Relations Board for 1966–67," *House of Commons Paper 437* (London: H.M.S.O., April 26, 1967). Proposals for amending and extending the law were made in the *Report on Antidiscrimination Legislation, The Street Report* (London: Political and Economic Planning, October 1967). Extensions, notably in housing, employment, and the provision of goods, services, and facilities were made in the Race Relations Act of 1968.

19 See *Report of the Committee on Immigration Appeals,* Cmnd. 3387 (London: H.M.S.O., 1967). A working group was set up as a result of a meeting on October 29, 1967, convened by the Home Office, "to consider how best the existing voluntary agencies concerned with the welfare of immigrants could join in providing advisory and welfare services as envisaged by the Committee on Immigration Appeals; and to submit proposals on the organisation and operation of such services" (*Report of the Working Group on Advisory and Welfare Services for Immigrants,* submitted to the Secretary of State for the Home Department, July 12, 1968). The Joint Council for Welfare of Immigrants was represented on this working group, signifying a substantial step forward in the group's recognition.

20 The issue of the composition of such a movement is frequently related to the structure and particularly the leadership question. For one view on the necessity of colored leadership as a precondition for success, see Neville Maxwell, *The Power of Negro Action* (London: Neville Maxwell, July 1965).

◉ Selected Bibliography

GENERAL TEXTS

Banton, Michael P. *Race Relations*. London: Tavistock, 1967.
A general analysis of race relations with material relating to
the British situation.

————. *White and Coloured: the Behaviour of British People
Towards Coloured Immigrants*. London: Jonathan Cape, 1959.
A systematic investigation of attitudes toward colored people
carried out in 1956, largely in areas where contact with
colored people was rare. Findings suggest, despite stereotyping,
that tolerance was a widely diffused norm.

Daniel, W. W. *Racial Discrimination in England*. Baltimore: Penguin, 1968.
Based on the *P.E.P. Report on Racial Discrimination in Britain*
and includes the same information.

Frankenberg, Ronald. *Communities in Britain: Social Life in Town
and Country*. Baltimore: Penguin, 1966.
Description of rural and small town life based on a variety of
studies with analyses of rural-urban evolutionary process. In-
sights into aspects of communities that are relevant to position
of immigrant groupings and inter-ethnic social relations.

Grigg, Mary. *The White Question*. London: Secker and Warburg,
1967.
A brief critical narrative account of selected aspects of race
relations. Part I deals with the United States; Part II deals with
Britain including impressions of local situations in a number
of cities.

Hill, Clifford S. *How Colour Prejudiced is Britain?* London: Gollancz, 1965.
A survey of 120 whites in four London areas with varying
densities of colored settlement relating to interpersonal contact
and attitudes toward colored people.

Little, Kenneth L. *Negroes in Britain: A Study of Racial Relations in England.* London: Routledge and Kegan Paul, 1948.
An excellent pioneer study of an urban community, the dockland of Cardiff, which covers many aspects of social relations between colored and white. Written before the recent colored immigration, it points out the extent of color prejudice and discrimination in a settled community.

Political and Economic Planning. *Report on Racial Discrimination.* London: Political and Economic Planning, 1967.
A survey, carried out in six areas of Britain, on employment, housing and services, and credit facilities; 947 immigrants were interviewed as were people in a position to discriminate in the above spheres. There also was situation testing using colored, white-alien, and white-indigenous testers. A generally high level of discrimination was found.

Rex, John and Robert Moore. *Race, Community and Conflict: A Study of Sparkbrook.* London: Oxford University Press, 1967.
An analysis in terms of the sociology of the city with particular emphasis on the "zone of transition" of a multiracial community in Birmingham.

Richmond, A. M., *Colour Prejudice in Britain.* London: Routledge and Kegan Paul, 1954.
Written before the recent colored immigration this work puts forward three interconnected hypotheses of ingroup/outgroup, status/security, and frames of references/communication to explain intergroup relations based on a field study of West Indians in Liverpool 1941–52. It was found that factors mainly responsible for color prejudice related to status insecurity and sexual jealousy, while discrimination was mainly due to economic factors.

Rose, E. J. B. and Associates. *Colour and Citizenship: A Report on British Race Relations.* London: Oxford University Press, 1969.
"A Myrdal for Britain while there is still time" was the initial idea on which this work was based. It became a report collated from many commissioned researchers into varied aspects of race relations in Britain that aimed to provide basic information, analyses of developments, and policy recommendations. A useful source book with bibliography.

MIGRATION

Davison, R. B. *West Indian Migrants.* London: Oxford University Press, 1962.

The social and economic background to West Indian migration. Included is a useful bibliography on the West Indies.

Eversley, David and Fred Sukdeo. *The Dependants of the Coloured Commonwealth Population of England and Wales*. London: The Institute of Race Relations, 1969.
An excellent summary of available evidence on the size and composition of colored Commonwealth immigration and forecasts of future immigrant population.

Peach, Ceri. *West Indian Migration to Britain*. London: Oxford University Press, 1968.
A detailed study of the determinants of West Indian immigration to Britain including data on the comparative economic and demographic situation in the various West Indian territories, geographical distribution within Britain, the effects of legislation to control immigration, and the degree of spatial segregation within urban areas.

Steel, David. *No Entry*. London: C. Hurst & Co., 1969.
A detailed study of the background and implications of legislation designed to prevent Kenyan-Asians, who were British subjects, from settling in Britain. Includes information on many aspects of racialism in Britain.

BACKGROUND STUDIES

Blake, Judith. *Family Structure in Jamaica: Social Context of Reproduction*. New York: Free Press, 1961.
A survey of ninety-nine women and fifty-three men. Material relates to patterns of sexual unions, family limitation, and fertility, as well as childrearing practices.

Eglar, Zekiye. *A Punjabi Village in Pakistan*. New York. Columbia University Press, 1960.
Gives a detailed picture of village life placing the emphasis on the ceremonial aspects.

Klass, M. *East Indians in Trinidad: A Study of Cultural Persistence*. New York: Columbia University Press, 1961.
A useful anthropological study of an Indian settlement in a rural area of Trinidad.

Singh, Kashwant. *A History of the Sikhs*. London: Oxford University Press, 1963.
An excellent historical treatment of the rise of the Sikh religion up to the time of the British pacification of the Punjab.

————. *A History of the Sikhs 1839–1964*. Vol. II. Princeton: Princeton University Press, 1966.

Ward, Barbara (ed.). *Women in the New Asia.* Paris: UNESCO, 1963.
A general background on the traditional patterns and changes in family life in Asia with essays on India and Pakistan.

MINORITIES

Banton, Michael. *The Coloured Quarter: Negro Immigrants in an English City.* London: Jonathan Cape, 1955.
A study in the East End of London from 1950–52 of a racially mixed area with problems of social disorganization. Includes material on employers' attitudes and interracial marriage and concludes that the major obstacle to assimilation was the attitude of the whites that prevented colored people from establishing normal social relations with the indigenous population.

Collins, Sydney. *Coloured Minorities in Britain.* London: Lutterworth Press, 1957.
A study predating the recent emigration but of relevance to the present situation. Comparative analyses of the Muslim and Negro communities in the northeast of England.

Davison, R. B. *Black British: Immigrants to England.* London: Oxford University Press, 1966.
An examination of the background and situation in Britain of West Indians living in selected areas of London. Material on housing, employment, and attitudes toward migration. Statistical analyses and case studies are used to assess the process of integration.

Desai, Rashmi. *Indian Immigrants in Britain.* London: Oxford University Press, 1963.
A descriptive study mainly concerned with Gujeratis with some information on Punjabis. The pattern of social and economic relations in Britain and ties with India are investigated.

Freedman, Maurice (ed.). *A Minority in Britain.* London: Valentine Mitchell, 1955.
Concerned with a variety of aspects of Jewish life in Britain. Particularly interesting for assessment of concepts of assimilation, separatism, and balance maintained between in-group solidarity and relations with wider society.

Gartner, Lloyd P. *The Jewish Immigrant in England 1870–1914.* London: G. Allen and Unwin, 1960.
An excellent detailed study of the processes of migration and settlement of Jewish immigrants together with relations with Anglo-Jews and non-Jewish English.

Glass, Ruth. *Newcomers: The West Indians in London.* Centre for Urban Studies Report No. 1. London: G. Allen and Unwin, 1960.

A comparatively early study of West Indian migrants including data on social composition, geographical distribution, housing, education, and employment. Attitudes of West Indians and whites in the context of the 1958 and 1959 situation with an account of hostile and tolerant political groupings.

Gould, Julius and Shaul Esh (eds.). *Jewish Life in Modern Britain.* London: Routledge and Kegan Paul, 1964.

The papers and discussions of a conference on Jewish life in modern Britain held in 1962 that covered economic and social aspects, relations to world Jewry, and the problems of research strategies.

Griffith, Wyn. *The Welsh.* Baltimore: Pelican, 1950.

A brief general text on Welsh culture and its relation to industrialization with the development of radicalism in religion and politics.

Jackson, John Archer. *The Irish in Britain.* London: Routledge and Kegan Paul, 1963.

The historical background to Irish settlement and an analysis of factors in the contemporary situation. The relations between the Irish settlers and the English is treated in terms of the political, religious, and economic circumstances surrounding the migrations. An excellent study of Britain's largest minority group.

Patterson, Sheila. *Dark Strangers: A Study of West Indians in London.* London: Tavistock, 1963.

Carried out in the late 1950s in the Brixton area of London. This inquiry seeks to document the development of intergroup relations within a particular social and economic setting.

Singh, Amar Kumar. *Indian Students in Britain: A Survey of Their Adjustment and Attitudes.* London: Asia Publishing House, 1963.

An exploratory investigation suggesting that adjustment and attitudes were influenced by a sense of inferiority about the backwardness of their country, past colonial status, and pride in ancient India.

Tannahill, John Allen. *European Volunteer Workers in Britain.* Manchester: Manchester University Press, 1958.

A study of refugees from displaced persons' camps who settled in Britain after World War II. A policy of granting educational facilities, housing (in some areas a share of subsidized council housing), and retraining the disabled was pursued and considered to be well rewarded by the economic contribution made by the European Volunteer Workers at a time of national labor shortage. Some material on national differences in patterns of adjustment.

Zubrzyczki, J. *Polish Immigrants in Britain*. The Hague: Nijhoff, 1956.
Historical background to the political and economic migrations from Poland and the Polish communities in Britain from the nineteenth century until 1939. An examination of the post 1939 emigrants' situation in terms of adjustment to Britain and the development of Polish political, religious, and cultural associations. Three types of adjustment, assimilation, accommodation, and conflict, are illustrated by personal life histories.

SELECTED ASPECTS OF RACE RELATIONS IN BRITAIN

Burney, Elizabeth. *Housing on Trial, A Study of Immigrants and Local Government*. London: Oxford University Press, 1967.
An excellent survey of local authority housing policies in areas of high immigrant density with proposals for action.

Butterworth, Eric. *A Muslim Community in Britain*. Church House, Westminister, London: Church Information Office, 1967.
A report on the relations between migrants and local people and between religious organizations. A survey of clergy is included.

Calley, Malcolm. *God's People*. London: Oxford University Press, 1965.
An account of Pentecostal sects among West Indians in Britain.

Conference on Racial Equality in Employment, *Report*. London: National Committee for Commonwealth Immigrants, 1967.
Papers and discussion reports on machinery for achieving equality of opportunity, both legislative and voluntary, by employers, trade unionists, and those engaged in immigrant problems.

Deakin, Nicholas (ed.). *Colour and the British Electorate, 1964*. London: Pall Mall Press, 1965.
The political involvement of immigrants and the impact of substantial immigrant settlements on native political behavior, including the election campaigns of the parties in six constituencies during 1964.

Foot, Paul. *Immigration and Race in British Politics*. Baltimore: Penguin, 1965.

An account of the attitudes and practices of the Conservative and Labour parties with reference to immigration, including a detailed study of the Smethwick election, 1964. Historical material relating to alien immigrants, particularly Jews.

Hawkes, Nicholas. *Immigrant Children in British Schools*. London: Institute of Race Relations, 1966.
A policy-oriented study of the problems associated with colored immigrant children and a survey of educational provision in selected areas. Largely concerned with educational techniques but some discussion of their effects on race relations.

Hepple, Bob. *Race, Jobs and The Law in Britain*. London: Allen Lane, 1968.
Written before the implementation of legislation making discrimination in employment illegal. Excellent summaries of discriminatory practices against alien groups before the recent colored immigration. The employment situation and main areas of discrimination against colored employees is considered against the background of possible types of legal control. Included is a useful bibliography.

Hill, Clifford S. *West Indian Migrants and the London Churches*. London: Oxford University Press, 1963.
A survey of integration of West Indians into the life of the Christian community. Includes data on six denominations in the London area. General conclusions are that church members (both professional and lay) were unaware of the problem and that West Indians were segregated.

Jones, K. *Immigrants and the Social Services*. no. 41. London: National Institute of Economic and Social Research, August 1967.
An investigation into the use made by immigrants of various social services. Concludes that immigrants compared to non-immigrants derive less benefit, partly because of age structure, and their contribution outweighs any additional costs in terms of health or educational needs.

Mandle, W. F. *Anti-Semitism and the British Union of Fascists*. London: Longmans, Green & Co., 1968.
A detailed study of the organization of fascists before World War II. Draws broader conclusions in terms of race and politics in the British situation.

McPherson, Klim and Julia Gaitskell. *Immigrants and Employment: Two Case Studies in East London and in Croydon*. Special Series. London: Institute of Race Relations, 1969.

Material relating to recruitment, promotion, relations between employees (white and colored), and trade unionism. The study of white-collar workers is especially interesting.

Oakley, Robin (ed.). *New Backgrounds: The Immigrant Child at Home and at School*. London: Oxford University Press, 1968.
Six essays by social scientists designed to inform school-teachers and social workers of the backgrounds of Indian, Pakistani, West Indian, and Cypriot children. Family life and the psychological problems of immigrant families are related to educational situations.

Patterson, Sheila. *Immigrants in Industry*. London: Oxford University Press, 1968.
A study based on fieldwork material of Irish, Polish, and West Indian immigrants in terms of phases of absorption into the industrial situation.

Wright, Peter. *The Coloured Worker in British Industry*. London: Oxford University Press, 1968.
A study of industrial integration of colored workers in different industries in the Midlands and the North.

PERSONAL EXPERIENCES

Collins, W. *Jamaican Migrant*. London: Routledge and Kegan Paul, 1965.
A personal account by a skilled carpenter of his experiences in Britain.

Hinds, Donald. *Journey to an Illusion*. New York: Heineman, 1966.
After ten years in England the author returned to Jamaica where he was unable to get a job.

Malik, Michael Abdul. *From Michael de Freitas to Michael X*. London: Andre Deutsch, 1968.
A personal account of black power developments in Britain.

BIBLIOGRAPHY

Sivanandan, A. *Coloured Immigrants in Britain: A Select Bibliography*. London: Institute of Race Relations, 1967.
A short but useful introductory bibliography.

◎ Appendices

Map 1

India and Pakistan, Showing Major Areas from Which Immigrants Have Emigrated to Britain. The Estimated 1968 Population for India was 524,080,000 and Pakistan was 109,519,831; the Estimated 1966 Migrant Population in England and Wales for India was 174,701 and Pakistan was 98,745.

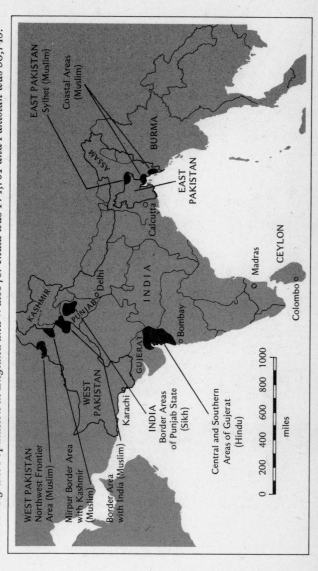

Map 2
*The Punjab of India, Showing the Areas of Jullundur,
Hoshiarpur, and Ludhiana.*

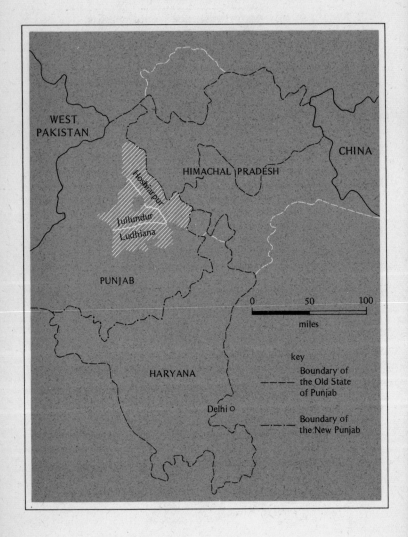

WEST
PAKISTAN

CHINA

HIMACHAL PRADESH

Hoshiarpur

Jullundur

Ludhiana

PUNJAB

0   50   100

miles

key

HARYANA

— — — Boundary of
the Old State
of Punjab

Delhi ○

— · — · — Boundary of
the New Punjab

Map 3

The Caribbean, Showing Areas from Which West Indians Have Emigrated to Britain. The Estimated 1966 Migrant Population in England and Wales for Jamaica was 169,156 and the Rest of the Caribbean was 132,976. Of Immigrants to Britain, 44 Percent Come from British Honduras, the Virgin Islands, Leeward Islands, Windward Islands, Barbados, Tobago, and Trinidad with a Total Population of 2,552,743 and from the Bahama Islands with a Population of 142,846; of Immigrants to Britain, 56 Percent Come from Jamaica with a Population of 1,893,077.

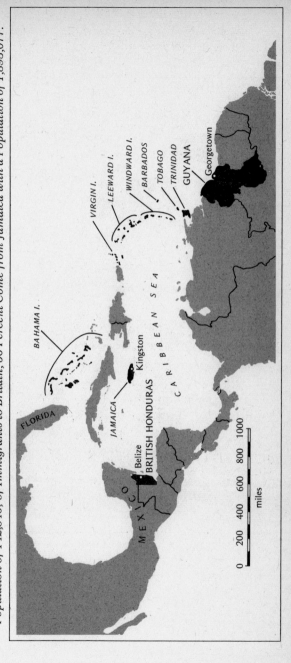

Map 4

England and Wales, Showing the Settlement Patterns of Commonwealth Immigrants in the Six Main Conurbations.

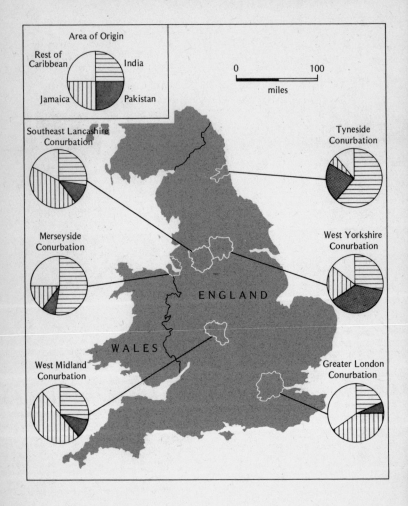

Area of Origin

Rest of Caribbean

India

Jamaica

Pakistan

0   100
miles

Southeast Lancashire Conurbation

Tyneside Conurbation

Merseyside Conurbation

West Yorkshire Conurbation

ENGLAND

WALES

West Midland Conurbation

Greater London Conurbation

Table 1A

This Table and Table 2A Show the Lack of Relation Between
Population Density and Emigration and the More Direct
Relation Between Economic Conditions and Emigration

TERRITORY	DENSITY PER SQUARE MILE	PERSONS PER CROP ACRE	MIGRATION TO UNITED KINGDOM AS A PERCENTAGE OF 1960 POPULATION
Barbados	1,398	3.4	8.1
Jamaica	365	2.4	9.2
Trinidad and Tobago	417	2.6	1.2
Antigua	501	3.1	8.7
Montserrat	369	1.5	31.5
St. Kitts	366	2.6	13.2
Dominica	205	1.4	13.3
Granada	666	1.7	8.6
St. Lucia	362	1.8	8.5
St. Vincent	538	2.9	5.3
British Guiana	7	–	1.3
British Honduras	10	–	–

SOURCE: Ceri Peach, "West Indian Migration to Britain: The Economic
Factors," *Race,* 7, no. 1, published for the Institute of Race Relations
(London: Oxford University Press, © Institute of Race Relations, July
1965), 33. Reproduced by permission.

Table 2A

TERRITORY	GROSS DOMESTIC PRODUCT AT FACTOR COST, PER CAPITA, IN PERCENT	1957 EMIGRATION TO UNITED KINGDOM AS A PERCENTAGE OF 1960 POPULATION
Jamaica	572	9.2
Trinidad and Tobago	822	1.2
British Guiana	455	1.3
Barbados	443	8.1
St. Kitts-Nevis	282	13.2
Antigua	290	8.7
Montserrat	203	31.5
Windward Islands	258	8.6

SOURCE: Ceri Peach, "West Indian Migration to Britain: The Economic Factors," *Race*, 7, no. 1, published for the Institute of Race Relations (London: Oxford University Press, © Institute of Race Relations, July 1965), 33. Reproduced by permission.

Table 3A

Estimate of Net Inward Movement to Britain from West Indies,
India, and Pakistan 1955–June 1962

	WEST INDIANS	INDIANS	PAKISTANIS
1955	27,600	5,800	1,850
1956	29,800	5,600	2,050
1957	23,000	6,600	5,200
1958	15,000	6,200	4,700
1959	16,400	2,950	850
1960	49,700	5,900	2,500
1961	66,300	23,750	25,100
1/1/62 to 6/30/62	31,800	19,050	25,080

SOURCE: (London: Home Office). Reproduced by permission of the Controller of Her Majesty's Stationery Office.

Table 4A

7/1/62 to 12/31/66

	WEST INDIANS			INDIANS			PAKISTANIS		
	Male	Female	Children*	Male	Female	Children*	Male	Female	Children*
7/1/62 to 12/31/62	−776	2,044	1,973	1,649	400	1,001	−444	10	297
1/1/63 to 12/31/63	139	3,666	4,123	10,757	3,074	3,667	12,852	1,341	2,143
1/1/64 to 12/31/64	1,457	5,467	7,924	6,162	4,154	5,197	3,713	2,108	5,159
1/1/65 to 12/31/65	1,215	3,862	8,323	5,510	5,873	7,432	1,046	2,485	3,896
1/1/66 to 12/31/66	−656	1,806	8,158	4,537	5,475	8,390	−914	2,707	6,215
Total 1/1/62 to 12/31/66	1,379	16,845	30,501	28,615	18,976	25,687	16,253	8,651	17,710

SOURCE: *Commonwealth Immigrants Act 1962 Statistics*, Cmnds. 2379, 2979, 3258 (London: Home Office, 1962). Reproduced by permission of the Controller of Her Majesty's Stationery Office.

* Children under sixteen.

APPENDIX III IMMIGRATION CONTROL
UNDER THE 1962 AND 1968 ACTS

This Appendix outlines the main legislative provisions for controlling immigration of citizens from other parts of the Commonwealth. The Commonwealth Immigrants Act 1962 confers on the authorities a number of discretionary powers so that some changes in the rules of admission can be made without new legislation. Where these have had an important bearing on entry or exclusion the relevant change in practice is included.

Part I of the Commonwealth Immigrants Act 1962 provides for the control of immigration from other parts of the Commonwealth. It is temporary legislation reviewed from year to year by the Annual Expiring Laws Continuance Acts. It applies to all British subjects or Commonwealth citizens, British protected persons, and citizens of the Irish Republic, except those born in the United Kingdom, those holding or included in United Kingdom passports issued in the British Isles, citizens of the United Kingdom, and colonies holding or included in United Kingdom passports, wherever issued. Control is not exercised over people traveling between Great Britain and the Irish Republic or across the Irish border.

Section II of the 1962 Act gives an immigration officer power to refuse admission or to admit a subject on condition of a restricted period of stay, with or without a condition restricting freedom to take employment. There is no general power to refuse admission to:

1. Holders of Ministry of Labour vouchers.
2. Wives and children under sixteen years accompanying or joining their husbands or parents. This includes step-children, adopted children, or, in relation to the mother only, illegitimate children.
3. People ordinarily resident in the United Kingdom.

There is no power to impose conditions on these categories for admission. Members of the second and third categories may be refused admission only if subject to a deportation order. Those in the first category, along with students and persons of independent means, including visitors, may be refused admission for the same reason, and, in addition, refused on medical or security grounds or on account of a criminal record.

In practice certain other categories of dependents, purely by way of discretion, were admitted without vouchers. They were:

1. A child under sixteen coming to join a close relative other than a parent
2. A son or daughter aged sixteen but under eighteen coming with or to join both parents or a surviving parent
3. The fiancée or "common law wife" of a man settled here
4. The widowed mother or elderly parents who are over sixty and belong to a person already settled here

The Ministry of Labour voucher scheme placed applicants into three categories:

1. Category A—applications made by employers in this country who have a specific job to offer to a particular Commonwealth citizen
2. Category B—Commonwealth citizen applicants without a specific job waiting but with certain special qualifications; that is, for example, doctors, nurses, and teachers
3. Category C—all other applicants

Applications in Categories A and B were given priority. Category C vouchers were subject to the condition that no country shall receive more than a quarter of the vouchers available for issue, and preference is given to those applicants who served in the armed forces.

In August 1965 a government white paper, *Immigration from the Commonwealth* (Cmnd. 2739), was published. No legislation has been presented on many of the proposals, but alterations in the use of discretionary powers have been made. These include the abolition of Category C vouchers, and, for Categories A and B together, 8,500 vouchers are to be issued annually, including 1,000 for Malta to be reviewed after two years. Category A vouchers are issued in order of receipt, subject to not more than 15 percent going to any one Commonwealth country. Category B vouchers are to be issued to people with certain special qualifications or skills:

1. Doctors, dentists, and trained nurses
2. Teachers who are eligible for the status of qualified teachers in this country
3. Graduates in science and technology who have had at least two years' experience in suitable employment since graduation
4. Nongraduates with certain professional qualifications who have had at least two years' experience in suitable employment since qualifying.

In February 1965 immigration officers were instructed by the Home Secretary to exercise the existing powers of control more strictly. This affected all categories where an absolute right of entry was not held. Students are admitted only for a specified period, which can be extended, if they were genuinely pursuing their studies. Certain dependents' categories were affected by the instructions to scrutinize the intentions and *bona fides* of Commonwealth citizens seeking entry. In August 1966 revised *Instructions to Immigration Officers* were published (Cmnd. 3064).

Commonwealth citizens do not require visas but may apply to the United Kingdom representative in the country where they are living for entry certificates. Holders of entry certificates are not guaranteed admission; initially they could be refused entry only on medical, security, or criminal record grounds, or "if it is clear that the certificate was obtained by fraud." Since the publication of Cmnd. 3064, the immigration authorities assume the holder to be qualified for entry unless evidence is found to the contrary.

The substance of the amendments in the Commonwealth Immigrants Act 1968 were as follows:

1. In the 1962 Act, the exception from control made in respect of "citizens of the United Kingdom and Colonies holding or included in United Kingdom passports wherever issued" was made conditional. The person or at least one of his parents or grandparents was either (1) born in the United Kingdom; or (2) a person naturalized in the United Kingdom; or (3) became a citizen of the United Kingdom and Colonies by virtue of being adopted in the

United Kingdom; or (4) became a citizen under Part II of the British Nationality Act 1948 or 1964 either in the United Kingdom or in one of the countries mentioned in the 1948 Act. This had the general effect of removing the right of free entry to the United Kingdom for many people. Because of the clause about antecedents born in the United Kingdom, the likelihood is that colored British citizens would be most affected.

2. Certain other amendments affected all persons subject to the 1962 and 1968 Acts and in general made entry more difficult. Admission could be refused to children under sixteen who did not have both parents or a surviving parent resident in or seeking entry with him to the United Kingdom. (Parents include stepparents and adoptive parents and either parent of an illegitimate child.) This section was most likely to hinder families in which the formal relationships do not give overall weight to the nuclear family.

3. Restrictions could be placed on entry in certain additional categories with regard to period of study, occupations, employment, and compulsory medical examinations.

4. It became an offence to avoid immigration examination upon entry or at least within twenty-eight days after entry. Previously a person had to submit to such an immigration examination by twenty-four hours after landing. Those people who transported the immigrants, such as the masters of ships or aircraft, also became liable to prosecution if they did not take reasonable steps to prevent evasion of immigration examination.

Table 5A
*Census Returns of Aliens in England, Wales 1871–1911**

		RUSSIANS	RUSSIAN POLES	RUMANIANS	TOTAL
	Male	1,724	4,385	–	63,025
	Female	789	2,671	–	37,613
1871		2,513	7,056	–	100,638
	Male	2,639	6,097	64	74,097
	Female	1,150	4,582	27	43,934
1881		3,789	10,679	91	118,031
	Male	13,732	11,817	437	115,886
	Female	9,894	9,631	297	82,227
1891		23,626	21,448	734	198,113
	Male	34,013	11,562	1,850	151,329
	Female	27,776	9,493	1,446	96,429
1901		61,789	21,055	3,296	247,758
	Male	33,312	17,289	1,992	167,762
	Female	29,550	15,390	1,730	117,068
1911		62,862	32,679	3,722	284,830

SOURCE: Lloyd C. Gartner, *The Jewish Immigrant In England 1870–1914*, (London: G. Allen and Unwin, 1960), p. 283. Reproduced by permission.

* *Estimates of Christian Poles in England and Wales, 1871–1911*

1871	1,500
1881	2,000
1891	3,500
1901	3,200
1911	3,500

Table 6A

Occupational Distribution (in Percent): Commonwealth and Irish Citizens Resident in England and Wales (1961) Born in Specified Countries, Males

TOTAL ECONOMICALLY ACTIVE IN CERTAIN OCCUPATIONS	ALL PERSONS (14,649,080)	IRELAND* (297,180)	INDIA (57,490)	PAKISTAN (13,430)	CARIBBEAN† (58,070)
Farmers, Foresters, Fishermen	5.1	1.8	1.6	0.4	0.3
Miners and Quarrymen	3.1	1.2	0.4	0.1	0.5
Woodworkers	2.7	2.9	0.9	0.5	6.3
Textile workers	1.0	0.4	1.5	8.2	1.1
Construction workers	3.5	6.3	0.7	0.1	1.2
Transport and Communication workers	8.4	7.3	8.2	7.4	11.5
Clerical workers	7.1	5.2	12.7	5.3	3.1
Sales workers	8.0	3.5	6.6	4.3	0.8
Administrators and Managers	3.8	1.9	4.7	2.2	0.4
Professional and Technical workers	8.0	6.2	18.6	8.6	3.2
Laborers	7.5	20.0	6.7	27.6	24.3
Remaining occupations	41.8	43.3	37.4	35.3	47.3

* Includes Northern Ireland and Irish Republic.

† Includes Guiana, Jamaica, Trinidad and Tobago, and other territories in the British Caribbean.

SOURCE: General Register Office, Census 1961: Occupation Tables (10 percent sample) (London: H.M.S.O., 1966). Reproduced by permission of Her Britannic Majesty's Stationery Office.

Table 7A

Occupational Distribution (in Percent): Commonwealth and Irish Citizens Resident in England and Wales (1961) Born in Specified Countries, Females

TOTAL ECONOMICALLY ACTIVE IN CERTAIN OCCUPATIONS	ALL PERSONS (7,045,390)	IRELAND* (152,660)	INDIA (23,630)	PAKISTAN (1,270)	CARIBBEAN† (31,540)
Textile workers	3.6	1.7	0.5	0	1.8
Clothing workers	5.1	2.5	2.7	0	11.8
Clerical workers	25.9	15.9	39.2	36.2	6.6
Sales workers	12.7	7.8	6.1	7.9	1.0
Professional and Technical workers	10.0	20.1	22.3	36.2	22.6
Laborers	1.3	1.8	0.8	0.8	4.3
Remaining occupations	41.4	50.2	28.4	18.9	51.9

* Includes Northern Ireland and Irish Republic.

† Includes Guiana, Jamaica, Trinidad and Tobago, and other territories in the British Caribbean.

SOURCE: General Register Office, *Census 1961: Occupation Tables (10 percent sample)* (London: H.M.S.O., 1966). Reproduced by permission of Her Britannic Majesty's Stationery Office.

Table 8A

Occupations of Males Resident in Twenty-eight London Boroughs (in Percent)

OCCUPATIONAL GROUP	ENGLAND	JAMAICA	CARIBBEAN	INDIA	PAKISTAN	POLAND	IRELAND	CYPRUS
Professional	3	*	1	14	10	7	2	1
Employers and Managers	9	1	1	10	11	13	3	10
Foreman, Skilled manual, Own account	36	39	33	18	11	34	30	36
Nonmanual	23	4	10	34	23	17	13	6
Personal service, Semiskilled manual, Agricultural	15	22	24	13	24	18	20	30
Unskilled manual, Armed forces, and Other	14	34	30	10	21	12	31	18
Number·	3552†	1389	1250	1097	211	1258	6143	883

* Below 0.5 percent.

† 1 in 25 sample.

SOURCE: From *Black British* by R. B. Davison, published by Oxford University Press for the Institute of Race Relations 1966, p. 70. Reproduced by permission.

NOTE: This table is based on detailed analysis of the 10 percent census relating to twenty-eight London boroughs made by Davison.

◎ Index

About the Author

Sheila Allen is currently Reader in Sociology at the University of Bradford, Yorkshire, England. She has taught at the University of Birmingham, the University of Leicester, and was a Research Assistant at the London School of Economics. She has made many contributions to professional journals including *Sociological Review*, *Race Today*, and *Medical School Work*. In addition, Mrs. Allen spent two years in Sarawak and has done research in East Africa.